Contents

Introduction

It is a privilege and an honour for me to serve as your President in this our centenary year.

Our industry has experienced a lengthy and consistent period of solid growth and we now stand at record levels of output and market share. Of course, over the years we have had our share of misfortune, but, overall, I believe we can rightly claim to have had a "Century of Success".

This book charts the history of the industry and of BCSA. It is published to commemorate the first 100 years of our Association and I hope that you will enjoy reading it.

Thanks are given to all of the BCSA Presidents who have served before me, to all who have been Regional and Committee Chairmen, to those who have served on Council, Regional and National Committees and to those who have, over the years, helped the industry via the Design Awards Scheme, Certification Scheme, Editorial Board, etc.

I thank our dedicated and hardworking staff, past and present.

Particular thanks are given to Alan Watson MBE for writing the early history section of this book.

Finally, I thank the BCSA member companies – without their continual support and participation, there would be no Association.

BCSA COUNCIL 2006

Donal McCormack

PRESIDENT

The British Constructional Steelwork Association Ltd

This commemorative book, original copy number 460

of a limited print run of 500, is presented to

Liverpool John Moores University

to celebrate the Centenary of the Association

June 2006   BCSA, 4 Whitehall Court, Westminster, London

A Century of ... ...tion

006

100 Years of Steel Construction

I am very pleased to send my warm congratulations to the British Constructional Steelwork Association on the occasion of its 100th anniversary.

Over the past 100 years, your products have become an indispensable part of the built environment in not only the UK, but in virtually every country around the world. The proof is there for us all to see in our daily lives – through new steel-framed hospitals, schools, transport terminals, power stations, bridges, water tanks, factories, offices, residential buildings and sports stadia.

You have a history to be proud of: from Tower Bridge in London to the Sydney Harbour Bridge in Australia; from Osaka airport terminal in Japan to the new Terminal 5 at Heathrow; from the giant telescope in Hawaii to water tanks in India; from industrial structures in Israel to power stations in China.

BCSA members are those whose technical knowledge and capabilities are regarded as amongst the best in the world. They have embraced innovation in all aspects of their operations. Their contribution will continue to be vital to achieving what we all seek – a world-class built environment, built by a world-class construction industry.

I wish you every success for your next 100 years.

ALAN JOHNSON

The British Constructional Steelwork Association Limited (BCSA) is the national organisation for the steel construction industry: its Member companies undertake the design, fabrication and erection of steelwork for all forms of construction in building and civil engineering. Associate Members are those principal companies involved in the purchase, design or supply of components, materials, services related to the industry. Corporate Members are clients, professional offices, educational establishments, which support the development of national specifications, quality, fabrication and erection techniques, overall industry efficiency and good practice.

The principal objectives of the Association are to promote the use of structural steelwork; to assist specifiers and clients; to ensure that the capabilities and activities of the industry are widely understood; and to provide members with professional services in technical, commercial, contractual, health and safety and quality assurance matters. The Association's aim is to influence the trading environment in which member companies operate, in order to improve their profitability.

A current list of members and a list of publications and further membership details can be obtained from:

The British Constructional Steelwork Association Ltd
4 Whitehall Court
Westminster
London SW1A 2ES

Tel: +44 (0) 20 7839 8566
Fax: +44 (0) 20 7976 1634
Email: Postroom@SteelConstruction.org
Website: www.SteelConstruction.org

Published June 2006
Designed and printed by: Box of Tricks

ISBN 0 85073 050 3
British Library Cataloguing-in-Publication Data
A catalogue record for this book is available from the British Library

Foreword

The historical development of steelwork in construction is a subject which has never been precisely recorded, because it came about as part of the general development in building techniques dating back to before the Industrial Revolution. Cast iron beams and columns are recorded as having been incorporated in the building of a five-storey mill at Shrewsbury as far back as 1797 and, by the middle of the nineteenth century, developments in the use of wrought iron had made it acceptable to Brunel and Stevenson in the construction of many famous railway bridges still in use today. The demand for ironwork in buildings then grew very quickly and, under its impetus, technical developments soon made supplies of the new Bessemer and Open Hearth steels available. The first rolled sections in this completely new material to be used in a steel-framed building in the British Isles were in a furniture emporium in County Durham, built in 1900.

The British Constructional Steelwork Association Ltd was formed in 1906 and is the national organisation for the steel construction industry; its Member companies undertake the design, fabrication and erection of steelwork for all forms of construction in building and civil engineering; its Associate Members are those principal companies involved in the purchase, design or supply of components, materials, services, etc, related to the industry. Corporate Members are clients, professional offices, educational establishments, etc, which support the development of national specifications, quality, fabrication and erection techniques, overall industry efficiency and good practice. The principal objectives of the Association are to promote the use of structural steelwork, to assist specifiers and clients, to ensure that the capabilities and activities of the industry are widely understood and to provide members with professional services in technical, commercial, contractual, health and safety and certification matters. The services provided by BCSA work both for the overall benefit of the industry and the direct benefit of individual companies.

The turnover of the industry is approximately £5,000 million pa with 15,000 direct employees and a further 50,000 indirect employees. The UK steel construction industry is the world leader and steel is the leading construction material in the United Kingdom. Steel's market share of non-domestic multi-storey building construction (buildings of two or more storeys) has increased from 33% in 1980 to an all time record 70% today. Steel maintains a 98% share of single storey non-domestic construction.

BCSA leads the development of the industry via a wide range of activities. The Association represents the industry on British Standards and International Standards committees; it operates the industry's certification and registration schemes; publishes magazines and technical and contractual handbooks; leads on health and safety; lobbies Government on the industry's behalf; and promotes the interests and capabilities of its member companies.

Derek Tordoff

DIRECTOR GENERAL

Chapter One - Before 1885

Retrospect

The history of Structural Steelwork, in common with the history of practically any other subject, does not have a particular starting point, and an arbitrary threshold must be chosen. After thousands of years of building in timber and masonry, it is only in the last quarter of the second millennium that metal has been used; indeed, it is only just over 100 years since any significant steel structures appeared.

Cast iron, wrought iron and steel have developed one from the other and each has been incorporated into buildings and bridges using continuously improving techniques. It may well be worthwhile, therefore, to look briefly at the beginnings of the structural use of metal and follow its progress over what is, after all, a comparatively short period of time.

Material

The so-called 'Industrial Revolution', it could be said, had its origins in the accidental coincidence of a number of happenings. One of great importance was Abraham Darby's discovery in the early years of the eighteenth century, that coke could be used in place of charcoal for smelting iron in a blast furnace. Cast iron became plentiful and cheap, finding endless uses domestically and industrially. It was easy to mould, had reasonable resistance to corrosion and had a formidable compressive strength, but it was unfortunately brittle and had poor tensile qualities. It must have seemed strange that, by using the same raw materials in another process, wrought iron could be made, exhibiting quite different characteristics. It was tough, malleable, had good tensile properties and

The first large span bridge in cast iron, Coalbrookdale, 1779

could be welded simply by hammering pieces together at white heat. Unfortunately, the production process was slow, output was limited and the end product was, consequently, very expensive.

So the alchemists went to work to find the philosopher's stone that would turn the now abundant supply of cast iron into a material with these very desirable qualities, in much larger quantities and at a more reasonable price. There were a number of false starts and claims that could not be substantiated, but credit for the invention that stimulated a huge increase in the production of wrought iron is generally accorded to Cort, who, in 1783, developed the puddling furnace. He also made another significant contribution in the invention of grooved rolls, which enabled all manner of shapes to be produced with economy. Some were decorative but the greatest importance to the fabricator was the rolling of structural sections, initially angles and tees. The puddling process was still, however, highly labour intensive and was limited by what a man could manipulate from the furnace to the hammer, usually about 100 lbs. These small blooms could be combined by forging or rolling but, even in the middle of the nineteenth century, it was exceptional to build up ingots weighing as much as a ton.

There was an urgent need for a better method and Bessemer, who was neither iron maker nor metallurgist, actually found something that he was not really looking for – mild steel. He was an able inventor and was trying to devise improved ways of producing wrought iron and carbon steel not, it must be said, for structural purposes, but to replace the brittle cast iron used in gun barrels. It was unfortunate that, after the tremendous excitement created by the publication of Bessemer's work in 1856, the process proved to be unreliable and it took two further years of experiment to establish that good quality steel could only be made from iron that had been smelted from low phosphorus ore. In the meantime, the iron masters, not easily persuaded that all was now well, had lost interest, which encouraged Bessemer to set up his own plant in Sheffield. Output expanded quickly, allowing him to fulfil his original purpose, since his steel was used to make guns for both sides in the Franco-Prussian war.

The initial problems with this process, and the suspicion that it created, retarded the adoption of mild steel for building purposes. It was 1863 before the War Office accepted it, but the Admiralty refused to allow its use until 1875, while the Board of Trade did not permit steel bridges until 1877. Meanwhile, another steel making process was gaining favour – named after Siemens, whose expertise, like that of Bessemer, was not in the field of metallurgy. His work as a furnace designer was taken up by Emile and Pierre Martin, who developed its use for steel making. Subsequently, Siemens himself, after a year of experiment, set up the Landore-Siemens Steel Company gaining, 20 years later, a contract for 12,000 tons of plates for the Forth Bridge. The Siemens, or open-hearth process was much slower than that of Bessemer, but each cycle produced a greater quantity of steel and the ability to use large amounts of scrap made the two processes comparable in cost. Also, the slower process gave time for chemical analysis and correction as the metal was being refined, leading to the claim of greater consistency and reliability. This process provided steel for the construction industry for over 70 years.

So, by the end of the 1870s, two successful methods of steel making were established. Confidence was restored, the industry flourished and wrought iron, which had held sway for most of the century, fell into decline. It is appropriate that in the final act, before the curtain fell, wrought iron was chosen in 1887 to build one of its finest structures, world famous, for being the first building to reach a height of 300m – the Eiffel Tower.

The huge demand for wrought iron had led to the formation of many companies engaged in its production. Apart from the ironworks, where each blast furnace might serve as many as 20 puddling furnaces, there were also many wrought iron makers who bought their pig iron and built their own furnaces. After all, the technology was fairly simple and the capital cost of setting up was not enormous. Not all of them, of course, converted to steel making because the demand for wrought iron continued, although in continuous decline, right up until the 1950s. Nevertheless, after Bessemer and Siemens had done their work, it was not long before there were in excess of 200 steel makers in England and Wales. The success of wrought iron production, indeed the world leadership, led to an unfortunate complacency and steel making in Great Britain started with problems which took nearly a century to resolve. There were too many companies operating on too small a scale, many with too wide a range of products. They were all fiercely independent. They suffered from nepotism, where management was a matter of relationship rather than ability, and they seemed blind to the fact that both production and efficiency were, in the USA and Europe, rapidly overtaking them. Bankruptcies, liquidations and amalgamations reduced the numbers over a period of time, but they were never sufficiently profitable to undertake the research and development that was necessary.

Even so, their problems were by no means all of their own making. As an industry which relied on continuous volume production, it was the most vulnerable to any economic downturn, leading to serious ills from fierce price cutting. Also, transport had so much improved by this time that there was an international trade in steel and our manufacturers were further embarrassed by low priced imports from countries which protected their own industries by imposing tariffs.

As the years went by, unbridled competition, poor management, violent trade cycles, wars and political interference all impinged on the British steel industry which makes it all the more astonishing that, late in the twentieth century, it emerged as a single, efficient public company.

Machinery and Equipment

It is very surprising just how much machinery was available in the middle of the nineteenth century, largely due to the genius of Joseph Bramah, not just as a mechanical inventor but also as a teacher and inspiration to generations of gifted men. One of his pupils, Henry Maudsley, a leader in the development of machine tools, also trained both Nasmith and Whitworth and, in the first 50 or 60 years of the nineteenth century, the science of mechanical engineering made astonishing progress.

This was the age of punching and riveting. Methods of construction were similar in buildings, bridges, boilers and ships, where components were built up out of plate and small rolled sections, mainly angles and tees. The constant drive for more economical production led to the development of machinery which would cut and shape plates and punch holes for the rivets which held everything together. Since plates were small, due to the limitations of wrought iron production, there were certainly plenty of holes and rivets!

In the heydays of iron

The Transept of the Great Exhibition of 1851. A striking example of the extensive application of iron for structural purposes. 3,800 tons of cast iron and 700 tons of wrought iron were used in the Exhibition pavilions

In 1847, Richard Roberts, who had also been a pupil of Maudsley, designed, at the request of Mr Evans, the contractor for the Conway Tubular Bridge, a hydraulic machine worked on the Jacquard principle which at one stroke punched up to 12 one and a half inch diameter holes through plate three quarters of an inch thick. Then, at the Great Exhibition of 1851, a shearing and punching machine attracted the attention of Queen Victoria who reported that it was "…for iron of just half an inch thick, doing it as if it were bread!".

There were attempts to automate other processes as well, sometimes as part of the continuing search for economy and occasionally to overcome the effects of strikes. Fairburn, in 1840, invented a riveting machine which, it was said, with two men and two boys could drive 500 one inch rivets per hour, thus making redundant most of his boilermaker riveters, who had been on strike because two men had been employed who were not in the Union. Radial drilling machines were patented in the 1830s and the twist drill, an American invention, came to us in 1860, about the same time as Mushet's work on tungsten alloy steel. Practically every machine that was to be found in a structural fabrication shop in the 1950s had been available, though perhaps in a less refined form, from the time that steel first came into use. Indeed, many workshops in the 1950s looked as though they had changed very little in 60 years, with their dirt floors, the cumbersome cast iron frames of combined punch, cropper and shears, simple hydraulic presses and heating – only on particularly cold days – by means of coke braziers. Methods, of course, changed, but not to the degree that might be imagined. There was a slow replacement of rivets by bolts as they became reliable and less expensive and steam was replaced by electricity, but the fundamentals were the same.

One aspect that is a study all of its own is that of the transmission of information. How, for example, did Telford, Brunel and Stevenson transmit their instructions to the workshops and to the men on site? Everything that was written or copied was done by hand, and drawings were not reproducible, such that it is hard to imagine the beautifully prepared details on cartridge paper being used on the shop floor. Checking the finished article could not have been easy either, without ready access to drawings. These are the factors that are not recorded, yet the introduction of equipment which copied drawings must have had a dramatic effect on production. The process of making 'blue prints' was established as early as 1837 by Sir John Herschel, but relied on the sun to provide a light source. The introduction of the electric arc towards the end of the century established a huge advance in one of the first examples of 'information technology'.

Structures

The early structural use of cast iron could well have been unrecorded props and lintels around the ironworks themselves, but Smeaton claimed to have used cast iron beams in the floor of a factory in 1755, and overcame the disparate values of tensile and compressive performance by designing asymmetrical sections, where the area of the bottom flange was several times that of the top. Another early use of the material was in the columns which supported the galleries in St Anne's Church, Liverpool in 1772, while in 1784 John Rennie built Albion Mill in London with a frame entirely of cast iron.

From the middle of the eighteenth century, the ironmasters, in their enthusiasm, turned their hand to making everything that they could from a material which was now becoming plentiful. 'Iron-mad Wilkinson', one of the most famous, made a cast iron boat and confounded the scoffers when it actually floated. He went on to build a church for his work people where the door and window frames were cast iron, as too was the pulpit. His only failure was in the casting of his own coffin, which sadly could not be used since prosperity had substantially increased his girth. But his greatest contribution, at least in the eye of the structural engineer, was as an enthusiastic promoter of the iron bridge, built in 1779, and which gave the name to the small town which surrounds it. The new material was slow to make its mark, however, and it is not until 1796 that Tom Paine, when not engaged in radical politics. which included writing 'The Rights of Man', turned his hand to bridge design. A frustrated export to America led to his bridge being erected in Sunderland where, with a span more than twice that of Ironbridge, it accounted for only three quarters of the weight.

Iron bridges might, for many years, have simply been regarded as curiosities, had it not been for the happy coincidence that Thomas Telford took up the position of Surveyor of Public Works for the county of Shropshire in 1787. Whether he was inspired by the original iron bridge, or swayed by the lobbying of Wilkinson, who became his firm friend, we know not, but he was not slow to realise the potential of cast iron, and became one of its greatest exponents. Telford immediately got away from the confused jigsaw puzzle that was Ironbridge and provided elegant designs with economy and simplicity of detail. As roads and canals spread across the country, cast iron bridges and aqueducts proliferated, many of which are still in existence and in daily use.

The first railway bridge in the world built by Stephenson on the Stockton - Darlington line in 1824

There was a demand, too, for factories and warehouses where cast iron columns supported beams of the same material with brick arches between them. These were the so-called 'fireproof' buildings which achieved popularity amongst those mill owners who had seen so many wooden floored structures burn to the ground. There were even examples where the hollow columns were used to exhaust a steam engine, thus creating a primitive central heating system and amply demonstrating resistance to corrosion which is one of cast iron's great virtues.

The Crystal Palace in Hyde Park, 1851

Perhaps the greatest demonstration of the advantages of mass production and prefabrication was presented by the construction of the Crystal Palace. in which was housed the Great Exhibition of 1851. Here, on a grand scale, the processes of design, fabrication and erection were co-ordinated, allowing the whole structure to be completed in an extremely short time to the astonishment of the general public. Perhaps the mass production aspects of cast iron influenced the builders and would doubtless keep the cost down, but it is surprising that more wrought iron was not used. Even so, Prince Albert was so impressed that he ordered a prefabricated 'iron' ballroom, which was duly erected at Balmoral.

The structural use of wrought iron was slow in development, largely because of its cost, relative to that of cast iron. Its tensile properties were certainly used to advantage in suspension bridges and quite a few, on a much smaller scale, were built before 1826 when Telford's Menai Bridge was opened. However, the impact of wrought iron was, in one respect, indirect in that its tensile strength made possible reliable boilers capable of higher pressures which, in turn, gave a great boost to the design and production of steam engines. Before long, in 1829, the locomotive steam engine made its entry and in the following 30 years, 7,500 miles of track were laid; viaducts helped to maintain reasonable gradients, bridges crossed innumerable rivers, roads and canals, and the mainline termini, the pride of the directors of the various railway companies, vied with each other in their grandeur.

Here were the opportunities that architects, engineers and contractors had longed for and they rose to the challenge admirably. There are many small bridges, some with cast iron arches and others with wrought iron girders, most of them beautifully detailed, still in use and largely ignored. The more spectacular Britannia Bridge over the Menai Straits, although substantially re-built after a disastrous fire, and Brunel's Saltash Bridge over the Tamar still attract visitors from around the world and the magnificent arch of St Pancras station, although completed later, in 1868, is one of wrought iron's masterpieces.

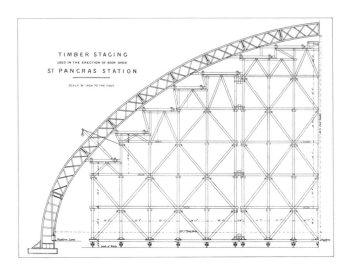

Chapter Two - 1885 to 1900

Urban Buildings

Although the use of self-supporting steel frames became the norm for industrial buildings, there seems to have been reluctance, in this country at least, to take advantage of the benefits that could be gained in commercial use. Offices, hotels and shops continued to be built traditionally, although steel beams made possible greater unobstructed floor space and their use as lintels opened up the ground floors and created the street scenes that we know today. In some ways, it is surprising that the urban American experience was so different. They had far more space than European cities and it might have been supposed that there would have been less urgency to build vertically. However, they were the architects who developed the potential of the metal frame in high rise buildings.

Wire rope made possible the design, by Elisha Otis, of the passenger elevator in the 1850s which, in turn, made multi-storey buildings acceptable to the general public. However, the complete metal frame did not appear until the nine-storey Home Insurance Building in Chicago was erected in 1883. Wrought iron was still in vogue and it is only the four topmost storeys that were framed in steel, which soon became, and still remains, the preferred material for tall structures. Even so, the metal frame was not immediately or universally accepted and multi-storey buildings in Chicago continued, for a while, to use load bearing walls, but as these approached seven feet in thickness at ground level, the supporters of the system conceded defeat.

Although the early American experience established the commercial potential of the steel skeleton, it was not to appear in Great Britain until

Redpath Brown built what is generally regarded as the earliest frame in these islands. The event has been given various dates, descriptions and locations – a warehouse in West Hartlepool in 1896, a warehouse in Stockton on Tees in 1898 or, writing in 1967, the President of the BCSA, J D Bolckow, claimed that it was a Furniture Emporium in County Durham built in 1900. The confusion was caused because, in fact, there were two steel frames, the earlier one having been destroyed when the building was burned to the ground in 1899. Furniture Emporium was correct. Its location was Stockton on Tees and it was originally built in 1896. After the fire, the owners, Messrs M Robinson and Co could only see "…bare walls, tottering here and there, with steel supports and girders twisted into all kinds of crooked shapes", but with great energy they set about re–building their premises. This time, they did their best to ensure that there would be no repetition of the disaster by installing sprinklers in every room,1,000 in all. Then, in an act that sounds like supreme bravado, they started a fire to make sure that the system worked! Before a large company of local dignitaries and the press, a huge bonfire of wood shavings and straw was set alight in the basement. Fortunately, as the flames reached the ceiling, the sprinklers opened "…in a manner very much alike unto a heavy thunder shower" and the fire was quickly extinguished.

If it is true that fashions are set in the capital city, then it is hardly surprising that steel-framed buildings developed slowly. It was not until 1909 that London County Council acknowledged that the thickness of external walls might safely be reduced should a steel skeleton be introduced.

Section Books

Dorman Long produced their first section book in 1887, setting out the properties of all the profiles that they rolled at that time, including beams up to 18 inches deep. Others followed, although there was no standard applicable and each company rolled sections which it considered the most saleable. Some time later, a number of fabricators also produced books of section tables incorporating all manner of useful data. Before any sort of standard or regulation appeared, these were the sources of design information and contained recommendations on stresses, factors of safety and loadings for various categories of buildings, as well as formulae for the design of beams and columns. Roof trusses, compound beams and columns with safe loads over a range of spans and heights, wind pressures, details of sheeting and glazing and the design of gutters and downpipes – all were included as people vied with each other to put together the most sought-after handbook, which would keep their name before the architects and engineers in whose hands lay the appointment of contractors.

Bridges

The 1890s saw the end of wrought iron as a structural material. Steel, made by the basic open-hearth process, had replaced it – quite painlessly so far as the fabricators were concerned. Their prospects looked bright: there were many factories to replace; developing manufacturing processes required structures and workshops, and the demand from overseas was undiminished.

The railway system in Great Britain was nearing completion before steel came on the scene. There were, of course, some exceptional bridges constructed in this period, crossing the Forth and the Tay, and there were still a number of less prominent bridges to be built or re-built and a few urban lines to complete, but these were 'tidying-up' operations, small in total compared with the booming days of railway construction.

Manchester Ship Canal

Between 1887 and 1894, one of the most ambitious civil engineering projects was carried out in the construction of the Manchester Ship Canal, where the entrance lock was 600 feet long and 80 feet wide to allow the passage of ocean-going ships. Railways, roads and the

Bridgewater canal lay across the chosen route, all of which were eventually carried by steel bridges. The main line railways could not tolerate any restrictions on the flow of traffic and were elevated on embankments before crossing the canal. Roads spanned the canal on robust swing bridges, which worked perfectly but were sadly not designed with the rapid increase of motor traffic in mind, causing endless frustration until they were supplemented by high-level motorway crossings. The Bridgewater canal produced a unique solution, where a complete section contained within a steel swing bridge could be isolated and rotated to let the larger ships pass. Although the ship canal is now little used, all its 100-year-old steel bridges still seem to be functioning as well as ever.

Towers

There was, however, one group of steel structures, which was hard to categorise — leisure complexes, perhaps? To some who visited Paris in 1889, it became a matter of national prestige that we should build something to rival the Eiffel Tower.

It was the enthusiasm and determination of Sir John Bickerstaffe, who at the time was Mayor of Blackpool, that persuaded the public into investing sufficient capital in the Blackpool Tower Company. In May 1894, the second tallest building in the world was opened to the public, who were hauled 500 feet up to the viewing platform in a lift made by the company founded by Elisha Otis. Not much above half the height of the Eiffel Tower and lacking its grace, Blackpool Tower has, nevertheless, basked in the affection of the public ever since. Of course, it was not just a tower since the base area was used for all manner of public attractions, including an aquarium, a menagerie, the world famous Ballroom, the immensely popular Tower Circus and an endless complement of bars and restaurants. Compared with 7,000 tons of wrought iron in the Eiffel Tower, Blackpool contains 2,500 tons of steel and a further 1,000 tons in the structures that surround its base.

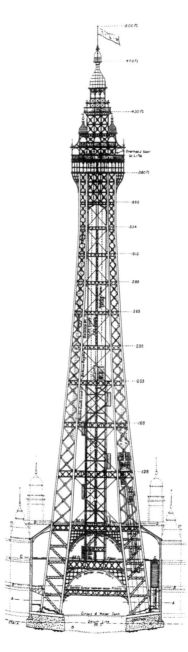

Blackpool Tower

Approaching the 20th Century

It cannot be said that the last 15 years of the nineteenth century was a period of continuous economic prosperity. However, neither were trade cycles as extreme as they had been, nor unemployment as severe or as long-lasting. Demands for steel increased both at home and abroad, shipbuilding enjoyed some good years and the steel makers earned a little respite from the uncertainties of the previous decade but, although our national production increased, its proportion of world output continued to decline as we were overtaken by both Germany and the USA.

Society was not totally devoid of social conscience. The first hesitant steps were taken in legislation to provide education for those who could not afford to pay, to prevent the worst abuses of child labour and to provide compensation for employees killed or injured at work, but seemingly nothing could be done to regulate the continuing trade cycles, which were the root cause of so many industrial disputes. After 150 years of industrialisation, we were no nearer to finding an answer to the problems in the relationship between employer and employee.

So the century ended with many problems, but with some hope and with one certainty – the structural steelwork industry was firmly established with a proven capability for the design and fabrication of contracts large and small, anywhere in the world.

Chapter Three - 1900 to 1910

Steel Making

Technical improvements in steel making had substantially increased production, indeed there was a growing over-capacity in the industry , which was also suffering from the advance in steel production in some of the traditional overseas markets. Nor were our manufacturers helped by the free trading stance of government, which allowed the dumping of surplus production by countries which, at the same time, were beginning to erect tariff barriers to protect themselves. Austin Chamberlain's unofficial Tariff Report of 1904, which was strongly supported by the steel industry, suggested tariffs of between 5 and 10 per cent, but it was many years before any action was taken. The steel makers had to do the best they could in conditions of perpetual fierce competition and, to some extent, worked together to stabilise prices. They also opened fabricating shops of their own as an outlet for their steel.

Of course, the actions of the steel mills were closely watched by the fabricators because they knew that, in spite of vociferous protests to the contrary, the mills were selling simple fabrication at cut prices directly to the general contractors. Equally, the mills knew that, in spite of vigorous denials, the fabricators were, at times, buying steel from abroad. In fact, this stand-off sufficed to keep both parties more or less in line with only occasional transgressions. There was, nevertheless, a deep-rooted suspicion, which persisted until the 1980s when the steel industry finally sold off its fabricating capacity, that competition was unfair because, it was claimed, those companies which were owned by the steel mills received their materials at a considerable discount.

The Fabricating Industry

More than most industries, the fabricators suffered from the peaks and troughs of trade cycles and, in the interest of efficiency, most of them reduced their 'all things to all men' approach and concentrated on one or another aspect of the trade. The simple truth was that there were far too many companies competing in the structural fabrication industry. The decline in the use of cast iron and wrought iron naturally led foundries and forges into the use of steel, with varying degrees of efficiency and not, in the overall, with much success. The effect, however, of only a small number of competitors who were short of work or, as has frequently been the case, were not aware of their own costs, was to drive the pricing structure of the whole market downwards.

Trade Associations

Against this background, the fabricators found it very hard to make a living. Not only did they suffer the self-inflicted wounds of under-pricing their work to meet the fierce competition, they also found themselves, more often than not, in the position of sub-contractor with the attendant hazards of 'Dutch auctioning', a device used by many main contractors to achieve rock bottom prices. To add to their woes, some of the main contractors were notoriously slow payers, while a few proved to be unstable and in the event of their failure, the fabricator suffered a financial loss with no redress.

Observing that the steel makers were benefiting from co-operation, involving some degree of price fixing, and that labour rates were fairly consistent across the industry, the fabricators made tentative moves towards creating an organisation for their protection. In 1906, five of the larger fabricators in the Manchester area put their heads together and, two years later, the Steelwork Society was formed, initially with eight members. The impact was not immediate, since there were many competing firms outside the Society, but gradually these people found that membership was to their advantage and 30 years later the organisation could muster a total of 40 companies in the Northern Counties. Similar groups formed in other regions of the country, ultimately to be amalgamated into The British Constructional Steelwork Association in 1936.

The minutes of the early meetings of the Society are anything but revealing. The only thing regularly and accurately reported is the passing for payment of stationery and postage charges, which is hardly an accurate measure of their activity. The substance of the meetings is only hinted at and it is clear that the members were uncertain of their legal position – to the extent of giving themselves code names and numbers. Reading between the lines, it would seem that their activities were fairly harmless, concerned mainly with exchange of information about wage rates and conditions and discussion on the effect of various pieces of legislation. Clearly, meeting and getting to know each other helped them to exchange small favours, but such arrangements were obviously outside the official business.

Design and Standards

In the first years of the century, design was left very much to the discretion and skill of the engineer or architect. There were no universally agreed permissible stresses or factors of safety, nor were design methods in any way mandatory. Reliance was placed entirely upon the integrity of the designer and it must be said that this confidence was very seldom misplaced. The incidence of collapse was rare and, as throughout the history of metal construction, the period of instability during construction was by far the most hazardous time. Nevertheless, when submitted to modern methods of analysis, some old designs, particularly the connections between members, have been found wanting, but the understandable ignorance of those responsible remains hidden by the factors of safety and by the forgiving nature of a ductile material.

The first steps towards regulation came with the foundation of the British Standards Institution. On 26 April 1901 the first meeting of the Engineering Standards Committee took place. As a result, BS 1 came about through which the variety of sizes of structural steel sections was reduced from 175 to 113 and the number of gauges of tramway rails was reduced from 75 to five. This brought estimated savings in steel production costs of £1 million a year. Steel merchant's costs were reduced due to fewer varieties. This made steel cheaper for the users so everyone benefited. By 1902, supporting finance could not keep up with demand for more standards. This led to the first Government grant and by 1903 foundations were laid for the world's first national standards organisation. This was a voluntary body, formed and maintained by industry, approved and supported by Government for the preparation of technical standards.

Between 1900 and 1906, BS 1, BS 4 and BS 15 were issued and periodically updated, ensuring that structural designers had at their disposal an agreed range of sections of a clearly defined quality.

The first regulations controlling design came in the London County Council (General Powers) Act of 1909, which gave detailed rules on permissible stress and loading and also, very significantly, made it lawful to erect "…buildings wherein the loads and stresses are transmitted through each storey to the foundations by a skeleton framework of metal…".

Buildings

It is not easy to define what exactly constitutes a steel framed building as, for many years framing was hybrid such that wrought iron beams, later replaced by steel, were used to span between load bearing walls. This system was followed by columns supporting a grid of beams, and this fully steel-framed arrangement allowed much greater latitude in the arrangement of partition walls since they had no longer to be vertically continuous. At this stage, all horizontal forces had, because of the restrictions of building codes, to be carried by external walls and it was not until 1909 that the steel skeleton, sustaining both vertical and horizontal loads, was permitted.

The Ritz Hotel, London

Here the trap is set of describing any particular building as "the first" of its type. It really does not matter, unless the structure had such an impact as to set going a completely new trend. The Ritz Hotel in London is often quoted, but in 1906 it would not have been permitted to act as a complete steel skeleton. It must therefore be said that there were a good many steel-framed buildings in various British cities which pre-dated it. A good example is the Midland Hotel in Manchester, built in 1903. It absorbed 2,000 tons of steelwork fabricated by Edward Wood, including some girders weighing in at 30 tons. One of the intriguing things about this contract is that it was driven by our old friend James C Steward, who had stirred up the building of the Westinghouse factory. He followed this by organising the building of the Savoy Hotel in London, which, in 1904, contained a similar tonnage, this time fabricated by Dorman Long.

Bridges

Growth in the use of steel was not confined to commercial and industrial buildings. Bridge design took advantage of the possibilities offered by the material both at home and abroad.

Our railway system had been developing for 70 years or more and the volume of traffic was vastly greater than could ever have been anticipated. Some bridges were found to be structurally inadequate and had to be replaced completely, while others were seriously in need of widening to take additional tracks. The reconstruction of Central Station, Glasgow required that the original wrought iron bridge over the Clyde had to be supplemented by a new structure carrying an additional nine lines. Although of economical design, crossing the river and two adjacent roads consumed 11,000 tons of steel – in other words, one fifth of the weight of the Forth Bridge!

It was uncommon to find a local authority with the foresight to use a rail bridge to support a road but, of course, there was the splendid example nearby of Robert Stephenson's bridge in Newcastle. The growth in road traffic was not foreseen – perhaps it was assumed that people would only travel short distances by car and continue to make longer journeys by rail. Whatever the reason, the fact remains that the road system in this country continued to use routes laid out by the Romans, with very little improvement for another 50 years.

Industry Flourishes

By 1910, the structural steel industry was flourishing. Standards had been set, methods of design, if not radically improved, had at least been clearly defined and the education of engineers was steadily moving forward. Workshop methods remained more or less the same as they had been for a good number of years, although here and there a well designed, purpose built factory was to be found.

Of course, like any other industry, there were peaks and troughs, although conditions varied in different parts of the country. In spite of the excellence of the railway system, work was carried out on a much more local basis, as is evidenced by the operation of the various trade associations. The Steelwork Society in Manchester, for example, debated whether it should increase its 'catchment area' from a radius of 35 to 40 miles.

Chapter Four - 1910 to 1920

A Decade of Disputes

In the years immediately before the Great War of 1914-18, industry prospered, unemployment fell and yet it was a period of industrial turmoil and unrest. Working people were aware that their living standards did not improve, indeed, in not a few cases they actually fell, and over-optimism in the previous decade produced a reaction of militancy, directed not only at the employers and Government, but also at trade union leaders, who were perceived to have become remote and compromising.

Some of the biggest and most bitter strikes that the country had yet seen took place in this period. The dockers and seamen in 1911 achieved some success, as did the miners in 1912 after a strike involving more than one million workers.

The Trade Associations

Companies, who had first made moves towards forming a society for their mutual benefit, were slow to organise themselves and it was 1910 before any real activity took place. Indeed, the name 'The Steelwork Society' of the first group only officially came into being in 1911 when the rules and by-laws were finally agreed by the original members. They were clearly a little uncertain about their position because their minutes record that each company was given a pseudonym "in order to entail more secrecy". In fact, these code names were not used since they found that the numbers they had allocated were adequate.

In essence, the group collected information about tender lists and where it was found that there were no outsiders, a tender fee of one quarter of one percent was added, to be paid by the successful tenderer into the kitty. Obviously, all orders had also to be reported. Although there was still a number of companies who either were not invited to, or would not join, it seems that the system worked tolerably well, judging, at least, from the sums of money that accumulated. Their activities did not pass unnoticed by similar companies in other parts of the country, leading to the establishment of the London Constructional Engineers Association in 1913, whose members were desperate to raise their prices and who complained that their work was too competitive and unremunerative. The figures quoted, which, it must be admitted, are hard to believe, are that in the 12 years up to 1912, the average price of steel was £5.075 per ton, and the selling price of fabricated work was £5.90, leaving 82.5 pence for workmanship, overheads and delivery.

Because of the intervention of the war, this group was comparatively inactive for some years, but it did try to set up a standard form of contract, which got to the stage of being drafted by solicitors, although there is no evidence that it was ever put into operation.

In 1919, nine companies in the Birmingham area set up the Midlands Association on similar lines to the others, reporting enquiries and orders. It was obvious that three separate organisations working in isolation would cause all manner of problems and some degree of co-ordination was necessary. The London group arranged joint meetings with the other two, which was the embryo from which grew The British Constructional Steelwork Association.

The regional groups continued to discuss amongst themselves the problems of wage rates and conditions and there is occasional mention of disputes. Certainly, they all had a difficult time in 1917 and 1918 when they came under pressure from the unions and when wage increases could only be authorised by the Ministry of Munitions.

Steel Structures

The whole construction industry and the shipyards were certainly busy as the Government of the day prepared for a war, which was thought to be inevitable.

As might be expected, industrial building, the mainstay of the fabricators, provided a heavy workload, but the methods of design and construction changed little. This was the age of the roof truss in its various forms which were used in a small number of different configurations – some, it must be said, with flair and ingenuity, but it was seldom that an industrial building warranted more than a passing glance, except to remark that new installations were on an ever increasing scale.

Not only were individual factories much bigger, but also there was a movement towards grouping them together and separating them from areas of housing. This was not necessarily a town planning decision, but a commercial development that offered an estate with all services and good communications by road and rail.

Even before the London Building Act of 1909, steel frames had grown in popularity. Selfridges, in 1906, which, surprisingly, in view of the complaints of the London fabricators, had a delivered price of £8 per ton, the Waldorf Hotel in the same year and the Morning Post building in 1907 had all contained a large tonnage of steel. The Royal Automobile Club of 1911 was a little unlucky insofar as it had been started before the 1909 Act and could not, therefore, be a complete steel frame. The same

Selfridges department store

could be said of the Calico Printers Association building in Oxford Street, Manchester, which was also erected about 1911, but it did have the distinction of being one of the earliest buildings with hollow tile floors.

One of the best-known buildings to take advantage of the relaxation of the 1909 Act was Kodak House in Kingsway, designed by Sir John Burnet and built in 1910. This was the forerunner of many office buildings and shops of ever increasing size. Australia House in the Strand, Portland House in Tothill Street and several office blocks in Westminster, Pall Mall and Oxford Street were built before the outbreak of war, as well as similar structures in the provinces. In fact, in a very short space of time, the steel frame had developed and was in general use as an economical and practical method of building.

Fire Regulations

When buildings were constructed of wood and the only means of heating them was by open fire, even minor accidents could lead to the total destruction of a complete neighbourhood. Local by-laws attempted to reduce the risk and were constantly reviewed and amended over the years as fire fighting became a municipal responsibility. The fire officers obviously had a big say in fire regulations and it appears that even though steel and iron were not combustible, they met with considerable opposition as building materials, on the grounds that their behaviour was unpredictable, particularly when quenched by a hose pipe.

In 1905, Rules for Standard Fire Resisting Construction were laid down by the Fire Officers Committee and although these regulations had no statutory force, they undoubtedly influenced many building committees.

Steel Fabrication and the Great War

Britain had not fought a continental war for 100 years; the Crimea was remote, as was South Africa and India and the scale of what was about to happen could not be imagined. The theory that the affair could be settled quickly by a brave and well trained regular army was soon demolished, but even so, the philosophy of 'business as usual' was adopted, certainly in the first year or two. Thus, we find buildings like Heal's furniture store in London, with a complete steel skeleton, being built in 1916.

Men from the steel fabricating industry served in every branch of the fighting services, with perhaps a proportionately greater number joining the Royal Engineers.

First, of course, they had to provide the infrastructure for the Army in France, building and maintaining roads, railways and port facilities and providing camps, hospitals, workshops and many other buildings.

Heal's department store

In the first few months, when the fighting was more fluid, it became obvious that the Engineers were ill equipped in heavy bridging gear and untrained in its use. This was a commodity new to the British Army, but the French had, for some years, used prefabricated campaign bridges, designed by none other than Gustav Eiffel. These bridges were composed of a small number of standardised elements, but were sturdy enough to support the passage of heavy artillery and were used extensively in Indochina. Later, they were adopted by the Russian, Austro-Hungarian and Italian armies.

The British also lacked military intelligence on which to base their probable requirements, but with tremendous speed they surveyed the bridges in northern France and ordered the necessary steel spans from the UK.

Special bridges, including pontoons, were also designed to suit a variety of purposes and loading conditions, and these were amassed in France while suitable training programmes were initiated. By the time that all this activity had taken place, the war had become static and the quantities of bridging material became something of an embarrassment. It was not until August of 1918, when our troops advanced and were frequently met by water obstacles, which had first to be taken and then bridged, that the training and equipment proved its worth.

Airship hangars, Cardington

Military installations had also to be built at home, amongst which were the hangars for planes and airships. Bigger spans were an obvious necessity; steel was the obvious choice of building material. One of the airship hangars built for the Navy in 1916-17 was 280 feet span, 700 feet long and 100 feet clear height in the centre and when the war was over,

it was used to build a series of airships, including the ill-fated R101. It needed to be bigger and the original intention was to jack it up, but it was found that, due perhaps to the lack of skilled people during the war, the quality of workmanship was anything but good. The decision was therefore taken to dismantle the building, correct any faults and rebuild it, 35 feet higher and 112 feet longer. This work was completed in 1926 to such good effect that the hangar at Cardington has almost become a national monument.

Chapter Five - 1920 to 1930

Depression Years

Depression settled on the country in 1920 at the end of the short-lived post-war boom. After the high hopes and promises of a better life, people became disillusioned with the values of political and industrial action and, in many areas, gave support to extremists.

The so-called General Strike of 1926 was by no means general, since it involved less than 20 per cent of the working population. Nor was it a strike against employers; it was a demonstration of protest against economic orthodoxy and the failure of Government to create a climate where living wages could be paid and employment maintained at a satisfactory level.

The Steel Industry

The fall in output between 1920 and 1921, distorted though it was by the miner's strike, was a disaster for the steel makers. Financially, they suffered a double blow, since many of them had also become coal owners in order to protect their supplies. They struggled on, unable to reorganise and with insufficient finance for research and development.

Once again, it was demonstrated that, in an economic downturn, the demand for steel fluctuated far more widely than the general level of activity. Also, in the 1920s, this was compounded by loss of exports due to the high value of the pound, and the level of imports against which there was no fiscal protection.

Factories and Buildings

Without doubt, the industry suffered in the general downturn, but by no means as severely as might be supposed. Quite a few developments were favourable, for although the overall building market was considerably reduced, steel frames had become popular and took a greater share. New industries were expanding, there was a growing demand for cinemas and football stands, for bus garages, for the generation of electricity, and for oil refineries with their attendant storage facilities. Indeed, although it is not possible to produce exact figures, it is probable that the overall output of the fabricating industry was rising. This was an industry with fairly low technology and a low cost of entry. Throughout its history, in spite of hard times and a number of liquidations and bankruptcies, new entrants have not been deterred and for the greater part of the last 100 years it has suffered from over-capacity.

City office blocks at this time assumed mammoth proportions. Imperial Chemical Industries, for example, built their headquarters in London, a fine building completely steel-framed with 6,500 tons of columns and beams. Many others followed, but they were not the only buildings to change the urban scene, for this was the age of the cinema.

Cinema balcony girder

To simply convert theatres to cinemas was unsatisfactory, since the theatre required so much space behind the proscenium that could be more profitably used to enlarge the capacity. Large, bright new buildings with seating for as many as 4,000 people were the order of the day, some using 1,000 tons of steel and every one presenting problems with the delivery and erection of the balcony girder. To provide a clear span of 100 feet required a huge riveted plate girder weighing 60 or 70 tons, which had to be manoeuvred through a city centre and lifted into place using heavy derrick poles.

The motor industry in the 1920s was beginning to take off. No longer was the car a rich man's toy; the Model T and the small cars made by Morris and Austin brought motoring to a much wider public, with all the necessary capital investment in new buildings for manufacture and maintenance. Road transport for both goods and people was growing rapidly and although it was still possible to find loads hauled by steam traction engines, the petrol engined truck was rapidly growing in size and number. Local Authorities found that they had to supplement their tram sheds with large span garages to allow the flexible parking of their fleets of buses. Here was a good market for the small to medium sized fabricators, since there was nothing particularly heavy in the structures.

On the outskirts of many towns, large steel structures began to appear in the form of football stands. By present day standards they were primitive in the extreme, consisting simply of what could have been an industrial building with one side removed and a few raked seats inside.

Electrical Installations

Up to this time, the generation of electricity had developed in a fairly haphazard manner. There was a vast number of power stations, many of them with a very small output, some direct current, some alternating, but even then, with differing frequencies. It is claimed that in the early 1920s, there were 43 different combinations of alternating current, direct current, voltage and frequency, varying from 25Hz to 50Hz and 100V to 480V. It is hardly surprising that it was not completely unified until 1947. It was, however, vital in the national interest that there should be some regulation to make the system conform to agreed standards so that power stations could be inter-linked to avoid total dependency on any one of them. In 1925, another Government committee, under Lord Weir, was set up and this time the urgency of the situation began to be recognised, resulting in the Electricity Supply Act of 1926, which called into being the Central Electricity Board.

It was not until 1927 that the national grid made any progress. An eight-year programme was proposed to interconnect and bring into conformity the whole of the electricity undertakings in the country, which provided a huge market for those fabricators who, with commendable foresight, had set themselves up to design, manufacture, test and erect the transmission towers that were soon marching across the country. Of course, before construction began, designs had to be established for conductors, insulators, control equipment and pylons, but in spite of this delay, the whole of Britain, with the exception of the area around Newcastle on Tyne, was linked up by 1935.

Trade Associations

Although the minutes of the meetings could hardly be described as comprehensive, they became a little more detailed and it is possible to gain some insight into the affairs of the steel fabricating industry.

It is very clear that everyone was worried about the shortage of work. Nowhere, however, is there any mention of efficiency or over-capacity. The only remedy that seemed to have had any consensus was that of protectionism.

More companies joined the associations reducing, but by no means eliminating, competition from non members, but many more tender lists contained members only, which allowed an increase in the 'tender fees' that were added. This, in itself, had consequences that had not been foreseen, in as much as a number of companies, colloquially known as 'fee snatchers', would do their best to insinuate themselves onto a tender list, with no intention of submitting a bona fide bid, simply in order to secure a share of the fee.

Discussions took place on matters of common interest – wages and conditions, daywork rates, problems arising from factory regulations, all were ventilated but the complaints of the members seldom resulted in a positive solution. On broader issues, members were made aware of the growing threat of reinforced concrete, of the damage done to the industry by the imposition of fire regulations and the necessity of propaganda to increase the awareness of purchasing and specifying bodies of the many advantages of using steel.

An often repeated complaint concerned the activity of the steel producers in selling simple fabrication. The problem was made worse by the agreements to fix the price of steel from the mills. Since the various steel makers could no longer compete with each other by reducing their price, a number of them offered the incentive of simple fabrication at what must have been considerably under cost. Soon they were also offering riveted compound beams and columns and while it may have appeared advantageous to fabricators to purchase from the mills, the truth was that by so doing, they reduced the amount of work in their own factories.

Tentative moves towards promoting steel construction were made by the propaganda committees of the regional groups without significant progress until, in 1928, The British Steelwork Association (BSA) was established, supported by both fabricators and steel makers, with the declared intention of promoting the use of steel for constructional purposes, by means of publicity, marketing, information and technical research.

The Fabricating Industry

In the turmoil of this decade, with a world depression, it must be obvious that the whole industry was fighting for survival. It is, nevertheless, a matter of some surprise to discover that the failure rate was nothing like as high as might be supposed, nor was it anywhere near that which occurred in periods much later in its history.

For this, there are a number of reasons, but first, the financial structure of the industry must be touched upon. Since it was factory based, there was an inescapable fixed overhead, which became all-important since companies operated on slender profit margins. It was also traditional that the industry took an optimistic view and calculated the overhead on the basis that the factory would be kept working at or near full capacity. To achieve this has been, over the years, a continuing obsession in the industry and the thoughtless price cutting, simply to maintain full production, has led to the downfall of many.

There were, however, alleviating features. Labour in all categories could be hired and fired at a few hours' notice and it was only necessary to retain those few key personnel whose loss would have spelt ultimate disaster. It was unlikely that others would be able to find alternative employment and were thus available as soon as there was any upturn in the workload. This is, of course, an over simplification, since employers were nowhere near as brutal as it might suggest. Many companies were privately owned, and the owners fought hard to keep a loyal labour force in employment, usually at considerable cost to themselves.

Private ownership also meant that companies tended to be cautiously financed. Investment had been made out of profit, which may seem a contradiction when it is also said that profits were low, but it must be remembered that the cost of buildings and equipment was also low. Unlike some later periods, therefore, bank borrowing was minimal, which, again, gave companies greater flexibility.

Chapter Six - 1930 to 1939

The Fabricators and the Steel Industries

The activities of both making and fabricating steel became so intertwined and the agreements between the two depressed industries so convoluted that it is difficult to comment upon them separately.

Across the nation, lack of finance brought about a standstill in capital investment with disastrous effect on the heavier end of manufacturing industry and on the building industry, though not to quite the same degree. The steel makers were, almost in their entirety, in the hands of the banks, but the politicians knew only too well that it was a national imperative that they should be sustained. The effect of harsh competition had not brought about the desired reforms and eventually it became necessary to protect them from foreign competition by imposing a temporary import levy of something like 30 per cent. This seems to have been done with some reluctance and was based on the requirement that the industry should "… show some determination to set its house in order".

For a long time prior to this development, the fabricators had been negotiating with the steel industry in an effort to end the strife caused by their so-called 'simple fabrication' activities. Eventually, a demand was made that there should be minimum prices for various categories of work below which the steel makers would not quote, to which the steel makers replied that the demand was unreasonable, since once their minimum prices were known, the whole fabricating industry would be able to undercut them. Indeed, the demand was only worth discussing if the fabricators were, in turn, prepared to accept the same conditions. In this way, the minimum price agreement came into being and many pages could be filled with the details of negotiations and of the complexities of its workings. It had taken some years to reach this position but finally, in January 1935, the details were in place, with the result that almost immediately the fabricators found their prices hardening, but it is not surprising that there were continuing disagreements, most of them between the fabricators themselves.

Technical Developments

The Steel Structures Research Committee's first report in 1931 recommended that a code of practice should be established for the use of structural steel in buildings and, with commendable speed, BS 449 was put together. Now, at long last, the designer had a nationally accepted set of rules and he knew, when he submitted his calculations to the local authority, that there was no reason for their rejection.

In the workshops, there had been little change since the beginning of the century. Processes were a little faster but equipment was, in principle, just the same. Perhaps the only introduction in 30 years had been pneumatic tools, particularly the riveting hammers which permanently deafened so many of the men who had to work with them. Developed in the late 1920s and early 1930s, the ability to cut steel using oxy-acetylene was a significant move forward and, being a process with very low initial cost, it quickly became universal. Some men developed extraordinary skill with 'burning' equipment and could cut sections, make remarkably accurate holes and even, by judiciously heating and cooling, camber a beam to a close tolerance. It was always said that you could set up as a fabricator with a garage and a burning set. Not quite true, for you needed one other piece of equipment which, starting in the late 1920s, has over the years changed many aspects of both design and fabrication – the electric welding set.

Welding

With the caution that we have grown accustomed to expect, the advent of welding was treated with some suspicion and made slow progress in design, in detail and in workshop practice.

By 1934, it was deemed that welding was sufficiently developed for the LCC Building Code to permit its use in structures. But clients were suspicious, engineers were unhappy at risking their reputations, and each design had to be scrutinised by local authorities who often demanded considerable revision. In any case, the economies that could be demonstrated were not very great.

Long after the event, many companies and many engineers claim to have been responsible for the "first" welded structure or bridge, but not one of them took a significant risk since early examples were all on a small scale. As early as 1931, a small gantry was built for the LNER in Darlington. It only contained 79 tons of steel and it is reasonable to assume that it was an experiment with a new form of construction.

Conscious of their responsibility to the travelling public, the railway companies took plenty of time to consider the merits or otherwise of welded steelwork, and it was not until 1938 that we hear of a welded bridge being constructed at Ladbroke Grove.

From the middle of the decade, welding advanced slowly but steadily, and most fabricators had developed some competence by the time that war broke out in 1939.

Trade Associations

The British Steelwork Association was partially funded by the various local societies and the fabricators were delighted to be able to claim some credit for the excellent work that had been done. Their self esteem,

however, turned to howls of dismay when it was proposed that the BSA should act as the co-ordinating body for the various local trade associations. The Steelwork Society, based in Manchester, had a healthy distrust of any organisation south of Crewe and held that this new body, based in London, could have no concept of conditions in the north. In 1931, a conference of the fabricating trade associations, along with the Bridge and Constructional Ironwork Association, approved by a narrow majority a resolution appointing the BSA as managers of their federation. The Manchester men were almost unanimous in their opposition, but were eventually led into the fold.

The BSA, now representing, and largely dominated by, the fabricators, guided negotiations with the steel makers in an effort to secure preferential treatment for members. This, the steel makers accepted, but only on the understanding that the local trade associations admitted anyone with fabricating ability. This led to a dramatic increase in membership, from 92 at the beginning of 1935 to 159 in April 1936. The local associations still retained some autonomy and operated to differing regulations, which led to disagreement between them from time to time. The Bridge Builders were somewhat aloof and the Tank and Industrial Plant Association seemed to hover on the fringes. It was clearly necessary that the common interests of all these groups should be adequately represented, that there should be some standardisation in the way that they operated and that they should be embraced by one organisation which could be affiliated to the British Iron and Steel Federation.

In effect, this meant an enlargement of the activities and authority of the BSA and the new organisation entitled The British Constructional Steelwork Association came into being on April 1 1936.

It was almost inevitable that, in bringing together such a diversified industry, difficulties would continue to arise, particularly over the workings of the minimum price agreement. As might be expected, many fabricators studied the fine print and either found, or imagined

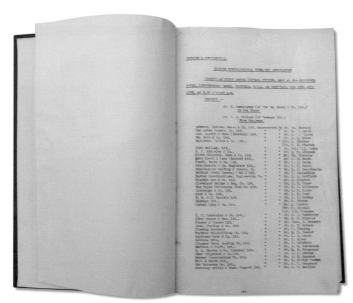

BCSA minutes book, 1936

they had found, a number of loopholes which they were glad to exploit to their advantage. The minutes of association meetings are littered with references to sharp practice and cries of 'foul'. In fact, many fabricators were found guilty of infringing the rules from time to time, but the advantage they gained usually far outweighed the penalty that was imposed.

Although its life was short, the excellent work done by the BSA should never be overlooked. Its initiative in research brought real economies to the design of structures while, at the same time, its promotional efforts, which included some excellent literature, were widely applauded. In these respects, the high standards set an excellent example for the BCSA to follow.

Industrial Buildings

One of the biggest developments of the time was the Ford Motor Company's factory at Dagenham, the first completely integrated motor manufacturing plant in the country. The new factory set standards of efficiency that surpassed anything else in this country, enabling Ford to make its smallest car with a selling price of just £100.

Power stations of un-thought-of size made good design imperative. Even though the national grid was well under way, power was still generated as close as possible to the user, and since there was a requirement for cooling water, facilities often had a riverside setting. Battersea, opened in 1934, eventually used 20,000 tons of structural steel. This can be compared with the 1,500 tons in the first Ferrybridge station, considered to be pretty big when it was built in the mid 1920s.

Battersea power station

Although the re-armament programme was slow to get under way, the middle years of the decade saw the beginnings of factory building and factory conversion for all the many and various requirements of the Armed Forces. Facilities for the construction of aircraft and their storage hangars both provided work for the fabricators, as did ordnance factories dispersed in some isolated parts of the country.

Shell building

Urban Buildings

The bigger developments, both public and private, were predominantly steel-framed in these years. Building of huge offices, started in the previous decade, continued apace. Two of the biggest, Shell and Unilever, both on the north side of the Thames, each contained 8,000 tons of structural steel frame and both were erected in less than five months, amply demonstrating one of the huge benefits of this method of construction. At the same time, on the other side of the Atlantic, the

Empire State building, with 50,000 tons in its frame, was erected in six months, setting a standard for the world to follow.

In buildings not quite so large, steel was also chosen for the frame, and perhaps one of the notable signs of approval in the middle of the decade was its choice for the new RIBA headquarters. This was a traditional riveted frame but instead of being restricted by cross walls, the occupants enjoyed the freedom of open spaces created by long span plate girders. Municipalities, too, took to the steel frame for their new buildings. Lewisham Town Hall and the Manchester Reference Library were just two of a type of building where the frame was more complex than the stanchions and beams found in city office blocks.

Hospitals, universities and blocks of flats all followed the fashion, but while this seemingly firmly established method of constructing building frames offered the fabricators a rosy picture of the future, they paid insufficient attention to the threat of reinforced concrete, highly regarded on the continent and making slow but steady progress in this country. Ten years later, concrete was given an artificial prominence and many more years were to pass before the steel frame recovered its share of the market.

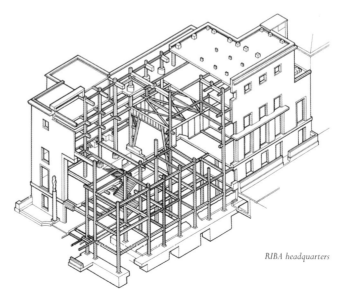

RIBA headquarters

Chapter Seven - 1939 to 1945

War

As Winston Churchill forecast in 1940, success against all the odds now enables the British people to claim, with justification, that this was their finest hour. Indeed, for a nation in continuous decline since the beginning of the century, the heroism, sacrifice and ultimate victory are amongst the few things that we can look back upon with pride.

The declaration of war in September 1939 was followed by some months of what the Americans dubbed 'the Phoney War', which provided an unprepared nation with some time to gather itself and to put into place the necessary orders and restrictions. Most industrial organisations had lost a great number of employees to the Forces, making the understanding and implementation of a string of Government regulations extremely difficult.

Those civilians who lived in the cities that came under attack had the nerve-racking experience of continuous nightly bombardment, but they were an unfortunate minority. For the majority of the population, there was full employment, very little poverty and a well organised and administered system of rationing, which spread the burden of shortages across the entire nation. There was, of course, a black market, but the patriotism of law-abiding citizens and a determination to share the sacrifices that had to be made kept its operation to a very small scale. To alleviate skill shortages, lines of demarcation were relaxed, women were allowed to train for skilled jobs when men were not available and many hard-won agreements were abandoned.

The Steel Industry

After the catastrophic trading conditions of the 1920s and early 1930s, which brought most of the industry into the hands of the banks, conditions started to improve as rearmament increased demand. Some companies were actually paying dividends by 1936, and by 1938 steel was booming, partly because the economy, too, was enjoying a modest upturn. By the time of the Munich crisis in 1938, many steel makers had substantial developments under way, a process which continued throughout the war, for these were prosperous years. This new turn in the fortunes of the industry was brought about largely by the price fixing agreements of previous years, conditioned as it was by an expectation that capacity would never be fully utilised. Of course, in wartime, every plant was driven to produce the maximum possible; indeed, some old plant that had been shut down was put back into use. High profits were made in spite of the severe problems that had to be overcome.

The Fabricating Industry

Virtually the whole of the steel fabricator's output was directed to essential work. Large tonnages were incorporated in new facilities for the iron and steel industries as well as in the maintenance and more efficient re-arrangement of plant. Consumption of electricity continued to rise, requiring additional generating capacity. The railways had to be maintained, as had all other modes of transport and the roads and bridges that supported them.

Factory building continued in all shapes and sizes, for essential work was carried out in small units as well as in the monster establishments built in some remote parts of the country and referred to as 'shadow factories'. Another enormous requirement was for aircraft hangars, of which three or four standard types were developed and put out to tender by the Air Ministry. Many of these structures can still be seen on disused airfields, some of them well maintained and in excellent

condition. In addition, there were constant calls for steelwork to carry out emergency repairs to bomb-damaged buildings and services, often answered with astonishing speed.

All this was traditional work with which the fabricators were completely familiar, but other requirements of a very different nature began to appear. At the lighter end of fabrication came the 'Table Top' air raid shelter. Many thousands were installed literally inside houses, providing a strong point around which the building could collapse without damaging those who were sleeping inside. There were, it must be said, those who preferred the rigours of the corrugated iron Anderson shelter in the back garden rather than run the risk of entombment.

Unlike previous military bridges, where the workmanship had been fairly simple, the newly developed Bailey Bridge had complicated all welded components made to exacting standards so that all were interchangeable. Parts were made in many workshops, encouraging the development of welding and the training of many operatives in this new skill, amongst them groups of females, accepted for the first time by the Boilermakers Society. The Bailey Bridge, with its great adaptability, was a tremendous success and was put into use in every theatre of war. It was used not just for conventional road bridges, but also for towers, piers and suspension bridges and, what is more, it is still being manufactured and exported more than 50 years later.

Most fabricators at that time maintained a fairly broad output and could turn their hand to platework as well as structures. Obvious examples are bunkers and storage vessels, where welding was beginning to take over from bolting and riveting. It was a short step for these skills to be employed in the assembly line manufacture of bodies for armoured cars and tanks. In a similar way, some fabricators found themselves making landing craft and later in the war, when so many merchantmen had been sunk, sections of ships, which were then sent to the yards for incorporation into hurriedly built replacements.

Unlike the steel makers, the fabricators made little new investment during these years. Apart from the growing introduction of welding, there were few innovations either in method or equipment.

The Invasion of Europe

After months of rumour and speculation, British and American forces landed on the beaches of Normandy in June 1944 and the public soon became aware of the detailed planning and preparations that had been made. Two complete pre-fabricated harbours, code named 'Mulberry', were towed across the channel and put together off the beaches to handle the 10,000 tons of supplies required each day. Inner and outer breakwaters were formed from a mixture of steel barges, concrete caissons and block ships to protect the floating pier heads, which were anchored a mile offshore and connected by a flexible steel causeway supported on pontoons. The total quantity of steel involved ran to many thousands of tons, fabricated in workshops all over Great Britain and requiring formidable efforts in co-ordination.

The BCSA

In 1936, when the BCSA took over the reins from the British Steelwork Association, there was already in place, in addition to the promotional and commercial activities, a technical competence that expanded to provide help to both fabricator and customer. The bridgework design department, for example, offered help to local authorities to the extent, in some cases, of providing complete designs.

On the outbreak of war, the total capability of BCSA was offered to the relevant Government departments who, on many occasions during the following six years, called for assistance in fulfilling urgent requirements.

At one time, the whole BCSA drawing office was engaged in converting ship builders' drawings into those more suitable to the fabricators' workshops. BCSA then arranged for its members to fabricate 30,000 tons of components for dispatch to the shipyards.

Mention has already been made of bridges and barges, hangars and hulls for armoured cars and the various works for Mulberry harbour, all of which were handled by the BCSA, which matched requirements to capacity and capability in the allocation of work.

However, the efforts of the organisation and its members did not stretch to financial support for the Government. Businesses still had to be run profitably since no-one benefited from patriotic bankruptcy and BCSA had many a tussle with the purchasing agents of a number of Government departments, who appeared to take a somewhat naïve view of the way in which a business was financed.

Wartime activities of the BCSA included much useful work in acting for the industry in negotiation with Government, not only on matters of payment and contract conditions, but also over interpretation of the many regulations that controlled the fabricators' activities. This naturally resulted in centralisation of power and a diminution in the role of the local associations who, nevertheless, still found that they had work to do in sorting out the often petty disputes which arose between contractors.

It is fair to say that the whole fabricating industry throughout the six-year period of national emergency performed with skill and determination. Within the bounds of the amount of steel that was allocated, all requirements were fulfilled, inexperienced labour was trained and ingenuity in design produced significant economies.

However, from the point of view of facilities, the industry found itself little further advanced than it had been in 1939. Workshops were in the same inefficient state, designed in days when labour was comparatively cheap, using equipment that had not changed in principle for 50 years.

One wartime development, however, was to have the most dramatic effect in future years, invented not for industrial use but as an aid to code breaking – the digital computer.

Chapter Eight - 1945 to 1950

Post-war Problems

The new Labour Government set about the singularly difficult task of returning a country, which had been totally committed to war, as painlessly as possible to peace-time conditions. At the same time, every effort had to be made to implement the promises of its election campaign. Mistakes were made, without doubt, but the six years of this administration had a profound and mainly beneficial effect on the country.

Most people who lived through these years will remember it as a period when everything except cheerfulness and optimism was in short supply. Domestically, even wartime rationing of a number of commodities persisted to the end of the decade, while industrially, there is little purpose in listing the commodities that were hard to obtain for it would have to include practically everything. One of the most intransigent shortages was manpower, since men and women in the Armed Forces were not released to civilian life as quickly as expected; indeed 'National Service' persisted well into the 1950s, calling up young men at the age of 18 or at 21 if they were serving an apprenticeship or were involved in further education. Also, people engaged on 'war work' found that, instead of redundancy, many continued to manufacture armaments against the possibility of war with the communist states.

The Steel Industry

Peace found the industry in considerable turmoil. There were those who, remembering the short-lived boom after the First World War, advised a cautious approach to development and there were those who wanted to take advantage of the elimination of debt, brought about by the high

levels of production during the war, and the prospect of profitable trading in the foreseeable future to create new efficiencies. On top of this was the promise of nationalisation, political interference over the siting of proposed new plant and the fierce independence of the steel makers.

But in spite of its inefficiency and the fact that it was operating old plant and equipment, which had been overworked for six years, it managed to hold on. The Treasury, incredibly short of dollars, had to find sufficient funds for the purchase of modern American plant, and in spite of all the factors weighing heavily against investment, companies began to carry out the plans for re-development that they had made during the war.

Nationalisation, when it did eventually come, was a half-hearted affair. The Labour Government was, by this time, divided on the issue – indeed, the agreement reached by Herbert Morrison that the Industry should be run under the control of a privately constituted Iron and Steel Board was later repudiated by a Cabinet committee. The delay in passing the bill through Parliament meant that there was insufficient time before the next general election to do more than take over the assets of the individual concerns and simply substitute the State for the original shareholders who, in general, were well compensated.

The Fabricating Industry

At the beginning of the war, the responsibility for regulating the prices of the various commodities that it had controlled devolved from the Iron and Steel Federation to the Iron and Steel Control, a department of the Ministry of Supply and consequently, since the Federation had been responsible for regulating the minimum price agreement of the fabrication industry, this too became a Government function. But with one significant difference – minimum prices now became maximum prices.

There is one further facet of the commercial arrangements of the

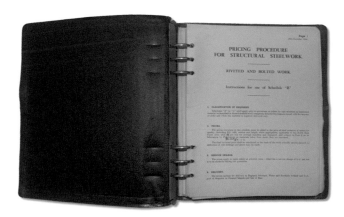

fabricators that has not, hitherto, been mentioned and that is the agreement dating from the earliest days of the local trade associations that all enquiries must be reported. Members were then provided with a list of those on the 'file', as it was termed, making it very easy to consult with each other as to any addition to be applied to the standard rates. Of course, conversations were not limited to this one topic and it was not uncommon for the members to agree amongst themselves which of them should put in the lowest price. On the face of it, this may sound to be a somewhat dubious practice, but in general it worked quite well, for the lowest price was not one that was inflated by the man who submitted it, but was controlled by his competitors, who were certainly not going to allow him any great favours. The other advantage was, of course, that such circumstances effectively eliminated the Dutch auction.

In spite of the good intentions of those who supported and arranged these procedures, it has to be said that price schedules gradually eased and, in a booming market, more deals were done. In other words, the system was eventually abused. It was quite common for the fabricators to quote prices that were absolutely identical and they had the naivety to suppose that this and other practices could carry on indefinitely. When the Monopoly (Inquiry and Control) Bill was promulgated in 1948, the BCSA immediately called in the lawyers but, strangely, were advised that, provided members complied strictly with the rules of the Association, they had nothing to fear. In spite of the omens that there were those in Government raising questions on cartels and monopolies, and in spite of public and professional disquiet over reports of the fabricators' antics, nothing was done.

Constant reference to competition, low prices, unfair purchasing practices and so on may give the impression that the fabricators were constantly on the brink of insolvency. Nothing could be further from the truth. Most companies had emerged from the war in quite good financial shape and it must be remembered that the minimum price agreements were pitched at a level such that even the inefficient could make a living.

Companies with good facilities and management prospered, in spite of the disruption brought about by the shortage of labour and the uncertainties of supplies.

Over this five-year period, trading returned to normality but not without a great deal of frustration, anxiety and sheer hard work in coming to grips with new legislation and the bureaucracy of controls. Companies were allocated a certain tonnage of steel and each building had to have a licence but, even with this paperwork in place, there was no guarantee that the required steel sections could actually be obtained. It was not unknown for substantial jobs to be delayed for the want of some small but important components, although difficulties were often surmounted by borrowing, substituting or re-designing. Delays were inevitable but the customers were extraordinarily patient – much too patient sometimes as the excuse of 'waiting for material deliveries' was used to cover other inefficiencies. It was certainly not good for the industry that the sellers' market lasted for as long as it did.

Political statements were often bizarre; for example, it was said that licences would not be available for industry or commerce since the whole building industry was to be diverted to constructing houses. It was also suggested that building licences should not be issued for steel-framed buildings since the steel content of reinforced concrete was less. This was the beginning of a war between the two constructional systems and, rather like the recent conflict, it was one sided to begin with, but the fabricators fought back and ultimately gained a narrow victory, although it took the best part of 20 years. Looking back, it is embarrassing to realise just how inefficient they were, but the fabricators actually thought that there was little improvement that they could make.

Although work at home tended to be of a utilitarian nature some excitement was allowed to creep in. The Festival of Britain used up 4,000 tons of precious steel in its main buildings, although it was not officially opened until 1951 to celebrate the centenary of the rather more grandiose Great Exhibition in the Crystal Palace.

The BCSA

Emerging from the war with considerable credit for its hard work and commitment, the Association now faced a period equally complicated in the introduction of new legislation and in the controls that persisted. Members frequently needed the sort of advice that entailed discussion in Government offices and the interests of the industry had to be furthered politically. Liaison with the Government Steel Control and with the steel makers was another vital task to try and ensure a more ordered approach to the sequence of manufacture and to the restoration of rolling programmes. Then there was the ongoing work in refining and administering the minimum price agreement.

The more responsible members of the industry were seriously concerned that all was not well and, through the Association, did their best to give a lead in what had to be done. Surveys were carried out in the areas of efficiency, education and training, but the lukewarm response from the industry must have been more than a little disheartening. However, work continued and was particularly valuable in the area of 'propaganda', which today we would probably call marketing. It was clear that the image and capability of the industry had to be projected both at home and abroad where the previously captive market of the colonial empire was beginning to disintegrate. There were some splendid glossy publications showing some of the very many contracts that had been carried out overseas and emphasising the size and capability of the Constructional Steelwork industry.

At the end of the decade, the Industry, collectively, had an order book stretching over a year ahead and had enjoyed, in spite of dire predictions to the contrary, five years of working to full capacity and at good prices. Prosperity brought complacency and the problems of inefficiency, lack of attention to training, poor contract conditions, competition from reinforced concrete and the attack that was about to be launched on the price fixing agreements, though not exactly ignored, were not treated with sufficient urgency.

Chapter Nine - 1950 to 1960

Time for Change

Certainly, the 1950s were pivotal insofar as dramatic change took place towards the end of the decade when the over-confidence, neglect and complacency of previous years led to a shake out of some of the less efficient companies in the first significant downturn in demand for 20 years. There followed a realisation amongst the more enlightened that re-organisation was needed in every aspect of their businesses if they were not going to follow their fallen brethren.

Additionally, the comfortable trading atmosphere of past years had lulled the fabricators into accepting conditions of contract that, in more stringent circumstances, were extremely onerous and which, even now, can cause considerable discomfort.

It would not be an exaggeration to say that this was the nadir of the industry. Everything went wrong. Inefficiencies in buildings and plant, in education and training, in productivity and labour relations, and particularly in management – all of which had been hidden by high demand and artificial pricing – were suddenly glaringly obvious and were exacerbated by the growing competition from reinforced concrete and, of course, the impact of the Monopolies Commission. It cannot be denied that there have subsequently been far greater upheavals and more dramatic downturns in demand, but at least in these later days the downfall of most companies was not so much due to their poor equipment or inefficiency as it was to their misguided commercial policies.

The decade was dominated by two problems: price regulation and steel shortages. Together with the steel makers, BCSA operated a (legal) scheme for the regulation of prices. The post-war steel shortages seemed to get even worse.

Price Regulation

By the beginning of the decade, the Government was starting to investigate all price fixing schemes and the BCSA's scheme came under increasing pressure. The Monopolies and Restrictive Practices Commission launched an investigation into the supply of steel frames for buildings and then came the Restrictive Trades Practices Bill which meant that the BCSA had to "register" its price fixing activities. This registration brought the whole of the industry's pricing arrangements open to public inspection. Next came a judicial investigation by the Restrictive Practices Court.

All efforts were put into keeping the price fixing as long as possible. The BCSA Council minutes record in 1956: "Those who remembered the conditions of the early thirties would agree that the industry should do all in its power to avoid a return to unrestrained competition and if, in the end, it proved impossible to avoid such a state of affairs, then something would have been achieved if it had been postponed for a period which might extend to several years."

It had been hoped that the Registrar of Restrictive Practices would concentrate first upon those industries which had a direct effect on the cost of living, but, because the structural steelwork industry had already been referred to the Monopolies Commission, the industry was one of the first 11 cases to be submitted to the Court. The Registrar denied all of the BCSA's justifications for the price fixing scheme and, on 18 September 1958, BCSA formally abandoned the scheme.

Steel Shortages

Members' order books at the start of the decade depended to a very large extent upon the degree to which building licences were granted for building in steel, as opposed to concrete. Because of the steel shortages, members were able to get less and less steel for use in building construction and the Government attempted to stockpile steel for use in strategic defence contracts. Rumours spread that the Government-owned nationalised steel makers were giving special treatment regarding the supply of steel to their own steel fabricating subsidiaries.

Output gradually drifted downwards: before the war it had been 857,000 tons and by 1952 it was down to 590,000 tons.

In 1952, the Government decided at a high level that the most rigid economy must be adopted in the use of steel in buildings and various pronouncements were made by Ministers that alternative forms of construction must be used wherever practicable. Architects and engineers were advised by the Government to re-consider their plans and adopt re-inforced or pre-stressed concrete. This set in motion a fundamental setback for steel construction, which took the industry another 30 years to begin to recover from.

German Competition

By the middle of the decade, exporters to mainland Europe were facing stiff competition from the post-war resurgent German steelwork industry. It was said that "the German fabricators were doing exactly the same as in 1938, when they were submitting tenders for work without any regard to the price but solely with the idea of obtaining foreign currency". However, it was also reported that when a German fabricator quoted an export project in Marks, then the price in other "hard" currencies was determined by the Allied Control Commission.

Technical

The revision of BS 449 was the subject of ongoing debate; during 1955 the BCSA's Standardisation Panel meet for three days in succession debating the changes. The concern was that the new version would add very considerably to the work in the design offices, and there was also the danger that the new requirements would be used by approving authorities as a justification for asking for a considerable amount of information which had not previously been given. There was a difference of opinion as to how far a British Standard should be regarded as a minimum specification and to what extent it should be extended into something in the nature of a textbook. In particular, it was considered that there had been inserted some very onerous requirements for laterally unsupported beams which were considered to be unnecessarily severe and BCSA agreed to undertake a series of full-scale tests.

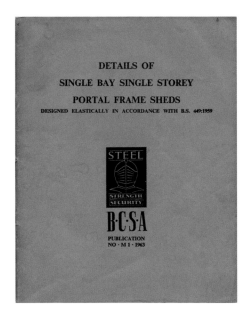

In 1956, the industry proposed that a Chair of Structural Steelwork be established at Imperial College, but whilst the College was very receptive of collaboration with industry, the College decided upon a Chair of Structural Engineering and a Readership in Structural Steelwork, as it could not see its way to confine the Chair to steel construction. Support was given to the course for senior designers at Cambridge University on the plastic theory of design.

The circulation list for BCSA's publications grew rapidly. The first of the series of new technical publications in 1949 went to 5,000 individuals – the enthusiastic response encouraged the Association to develop more publications and by 1952 the circulation was up to 18,500. By 1955, when the demand had reached 22,000 per book, a nominal charge of 2/6d per copy was introduced.

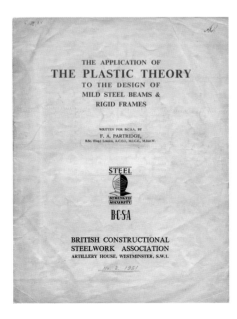

In 1953, a journalist was engaged to provide editorial material for the national and local press in relation to any subject in which the efficacy of steel could be introduced. The first of these articles was published in the "Recorder" on 12 June 1954. A four-page leaflet was also produced for members exhibiting at the Royal Show in Windsor in 1953.

Study Visit to the USA

BCSA encouraged the industry to look outwards and in 1951 a study team set sail for New York – "on the boat out the team was split up into sections of those specialising in the various subjects". The conclusions of the visit were:

"Production is higher in the USA but this is not solely due to more strenuous physical effort on the part of labour, although there is a greater sustained effort on the part of operatives, with no sit down breaks for tea, etc. It is rather the result of the co-ordination of that sustained effort brought about by management, planning, high quality of executives and foremen, provision of handling devices to a greater extent than here and, particularly, by the realisation and acceptance by management, executives, trade unions and labour that high production is in the best interests of all to counter by reducing costs what is undoubtedly the high cost of living in the USA.

"Other main contributing labour issues were: (a) acceptance by the unions and operatives of time study of operations; (b) a single union for each works; (c) the employer's right to engage labour without restriction, providing the entrant agrees to join a union; (d) absence of demarcation.

"Key points were: (a) the great range of wide flange beams available; (b) the use of automatic punching machines instead of drilling; (c) the absence of cold saws – beams either being cut to length at the mills or burned to length in the works; (d) phenomenal rate of pom pom riveting – at one Bethlehem works, 2,000 rivets per shift were driven.

"The Americans have appreciated the psychological effect of colour painting of shops, general cleanliness and tidiness. Earth floors were exceptional.

"Site erection is faster, with extensive use of Caterpillar cranes with jibs up to 120 feet used for skyscrapers up to the limit of their reach with subsequent use of jumping guyed derricks."

The Chairman of the Study Team concluded:

"May I suggest here that, as one who is now approaching old age, the time has arrived at which, as I have personally advocated before, there should be a Junior BCSA of the younger Members of the Industry and that this Report on the American Industry should be their Bible. The time has arrived when we should give greater encouragement to the younger people in our Industry."

Chapter Ten - 1960 to 1970

A New Promotion Campaign

For the start of the new decade, BCSA, together with the steel makers, launched a new 'Joint Propaganda Project', involving new staff, new brochures, a magazine, a programme of works visits, etc. "Building With Steel" commenced publication in February 1960 with a circulation of 15,000 copies.

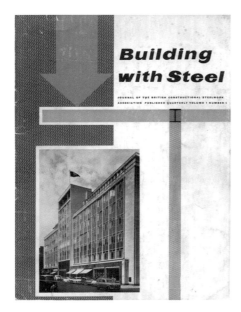

The tacit agreement between 'steel' and 'concrete' not to cite the other materials in their 'propaganda' started to break down in 1961 when a leaflet "Why Choose Concrete" drew comparisons between concrete and steel.

A group of architects was taken to Paris in 1962 to see steel-framed buildings being erected and the extent to which no fire protection was being applied. By 1962, BCSA's annual promotion spend had reached £96,000 – equivalent to £1.4 million at 2006 values and five times more than the current spend.

In 1963, there were 62,000 technical brochures published, 58,000 pamphlets for engineers and architects and 86,000 copies of "Building With Steel".

However, by 1965, unfavourable comparisons were being drawn by members and others to the increasing activities of the Cement & Concrete Association (C&CA); designs were being converted from steel to concrete on the grounds of cost and speed of erection. "BCSA is unable to come to terms with basic problems and its obvious lack of imagination," said one member.

An export Group was established in 1966, with an Export Director who made extensive overseas visits to Conferences and Exhibitions to promote the British structural steelwork industry.

What was to become the industry's ongoing flagship promotion event, the Structural Steel Design Awards Scheme, was established in 1969 and 40 entries were received in the first year.

Technical Developments

In the late 1950s and early 1960s, three major developments helped the industry:

- the introduction of high strength bolts – one result of the combined effect of high strength bolts and arc welding was to virtually eliminate rivetting, both in the fabrication shop and on site.

- the rolling of Universal Beam and Column sizes – when introduced in 1962 immediately increased the ability to compete in overseas markets.

- the development in the use of digital computing in engineering – the computer provided a powerful tool to both designer and draughtsman. In the beginning, this was used for the analysis of rigid frames, thus enabling the true potential of electric arc welding to be fully appreciated.

The new section range in 1962, together with increased yield strengths, necessitated the development and publication of a new set of safe load tables. Further new technical publications continued to be produced, eg "Deflection of Portal Frames".

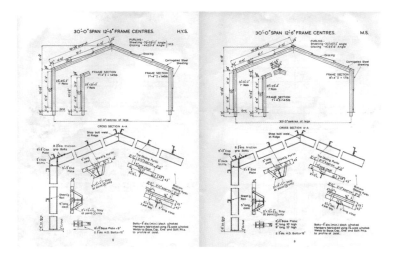

The results of an investigation into the economics of alternative methods of fire protection were published in 1961, viz "Modern Fire Protection for Structural Steelwork" and BCSA encouraged the formation of the Structural Steelwork Fire Protection Association in order to promote lightweight protection systems. A series of full-scale fire tests was carried out at the Fire Research Station in 1964.

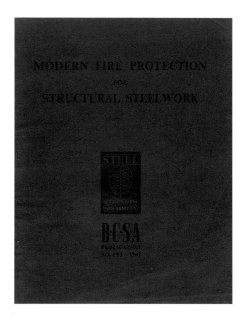

BCSA recognised the benefits of University links and in 1966 sponsored a programme of research at the Universities of Cambridge, Swansea and Newcastle and at Imperial College.

During the 1960s, BCSA developed a bridge department, which established a worldwide reputation for its design advisory service.

In 1967, a heavy involvement took place in the changeover to the metric system and this necessitated the production and printing in metric of many publications, eg the Safe Load Tables and "Metric Practice", plus courses for members.

A special working party was established in 1968 to determine the types of weathering steel which could be made available.

By 1969, BCSA had established a Computer Design Service, through which members could "obtain scantlings for single bay portal frames under various loading conditions within 24 hours".

Commercial

The decline in the industry's output which took place in the 1950s continued into the 1960s. By 1962, too much capacity was chasing too few orders: capacity had increased due to the installation of new fabricating machinery plus competition from concrete reduced the available steelwork. There was concern that some companies were quoting prices at below cost. It was noted that in Australia steel dominated the multi-storey market, whereas in the UK it was now concrete due, it was claimed, to steel prices being too high. The industry's output averaged 700,000 tons pa during the 1960s.

BCSA joined forces with HVCA and ECA in 1962 to create CASEC (Confederation of Associations of Specialist Engineering Contractors) to represent the specialist contractors on the Joint Construction Committee, the Joint Contracts Tribunal, etc.

Negotiations took place with the Central Electricity Generating Board (CEGB) regarding steelwork measurement and payment terms on power station contracts.

By the middle of the decade, fears emerged that the nationalisation of the steel companies would also impinge on the steelwork fabrication industry, as 25% of the industry's output was produced by the fabrication subsidiaries of the steel makers.

In 1967, BCSA established a legal advisory service to give members contractual advice and to develop contractual forms, eg a standard form of indemnity for the early release of retentions.

Chapter Eleven - 1970 to 1980

Industry Output

By the early 1970s, industry order books were in a healthier state due to an upsurge in demand. Some frustrations though existed for steelwork contractors due to the long delivery dates that were quoted by the rolling mills. Improved trading conditions were expected to continue for some time, but an inflationary spiral gripped the country and precipitated demands for substantial increases in wages and salaries, and also exceptional increases in the cost of raw steel and of other materials, thus creating problems for steelwork fabricators.

In 1972, the UK entered the European Economic Community and the BCSA achieved closer ties with Continental steel makers through the European Commission and the European Convention for Constructional Steelwork. Closer and more practical liaison was established with the British steel makers with regard to steel mills' performance, steel qualities, prices and the basing point system.

1974 saw the long awaited cyclical recovery; confidence was buoyant. The steel industry had been nationalised in 1966 and the resulting British Steel Corporation agreed plans with the BCSA to ensure a steady build-up of supplies for steelwork fabricators in spite of the worldwide demand for steel which had developed. At home the new Corporation had ambitious plans itself for increasing and modernising its steel making capacity, including one scheme – Anchor – that alone required 40,000 tonnes of steelwork at Scunthorpe. Several schemes were only part-complete when the short-lived optimism was dealt a double blow of suddenly increased oil prices and of serious industrial disputes, leading to the three-day power week and a change in Government. This was a testing time for both the steelwork fabricators and the BCSA. The legacy

in terms of the UK steel industry was that it had some modern facilities, most notably the continuous casting process that provided much better quality products. Other investments languished, such that the second blast furnace for Redcar lay in pieces for many years until it was sold eventually to Brazil.

1979/1980 was the worst year (known at that time) since the 1930s in the structural steelwork industry. A worsening economic climate, accompanied by two severe periods of industrial disruption, hit the fabricators hard. There was a three-month engineering dispute which reduced working to three days per week, and this was followed by a total strike in the British Steel Corporation that completely stopped production of fabricators' basic raw material for three months. Many companies ceased to trade either voluntarily or by forced closure. Those fabricators remaining faced a fiercely competitive situation with uneconomic price levels and severe financial pressures.

Technical

BCSA's fortunes suffered at the turn the decade, along with those of the industry, and it became necessary to reduce the levy paid by members by 40%. Costs needed to be cut and, following discussions with the British Steel Corporation, CONSTRADO (Constructional Steel Research and Development Organisation) was formed in the early part of 1971 as a new "independent" technical organisation (to be funded by the British Steel Corporation). Certain of the BCSA's technical staff, including the Technical Director, were transferred to CONSTRADO. Whilst some of BCSA's technical activities, eg education, bridge design department, sponsorship of University research, etc were transferred to CONSTRADO, it was recognised that BCSA needed to retain a core technical expertise to represent the industry on technical issues such as Building Regulations, welding, computers, etc and to advise members on technical matters.

BCSA's cost study of multi-storey buildings project resulted in the devising of a method of construction for application to a range of office buildings of up to nine storeys in height, incorporating a low-cost fire protection system.

The Appraisal Rules issued by the Merrison Committee in the early 1970s after the collapse during erection of certain box girder bridges gave rise to considerable concern amongst the bridgework fabricators; the arduous requirements of the rules led to the establishment of a working party on tolerances. Subsequently, BCSA became extensively involved in the drafting of the new limit state rules in BS 5400 for design and fabrication to ensure that steel bridges continued to be safe and economical to construct.

Similarly, the Association was involved in the middle of the decade in the early stages of the revision of BS 449 (later to become BS 5950) "so that the thinking in that regard could be considered and in order also to ensure that the proposed adoption of limit state design was kept within practical bounds".

In 1977, the ECCS Recommendations on the Design of Constructional Steelwork were published and it was proposed by the European Commission that they "be adopted as the model for the new Eurocodes".

BCSA's Industrial Training Advisor regularly visited member companies to advise members on training courses and to advise members on grants from the Engineering Industry Training Board.

1976 – an Olivetti P652 computer running a program for portal frame design.

Contractual

At the start of the decade, BCSA published its Conditions of Sale for Structural Steelwork for use by members incorporating improved payment terms, in particular, progress payments for black steel and for fabricated material stored at works. These, and also BCSA's new model fluctuation clauses, were registered with the Register of Restrictive Trading Agreements.

The Scheme for Interfirm Comparisons enabled members to compare their costs of fabrication and their profitability levels. The first edition of the Members' Contractual Handbook was published in 1973.

Payment terms were an ongoing concern and in 1976 BCSA reached agreement with the Government to increase the proportion of the value of payment for materials delivered to site to 97%. Continued pressure was also maintained for the introduction of provisions allowing for the early release of retentions to steelwork contractors who frequently had to wait months, even years, before their entitlement was paid over. Members doing fabrication work for the British Steel Corporation had to accept a retentions rate of 20%.

During 1979, BCSA introduced its Professional Indemnity insurance scheme for members.

"Specify Steel"

In 1975, a new promotion campaign was launched called "Specify Steel" to help remedy the fall-off in members' order books. The campaign opened with a co-ordinated advertisement in the Financial Times on 25 March, together with an editorial supplement. The core of the new campaign was a series of promotional publications in several languages, incorporating the campaign logo and demonstrating members' achievements in various market sectors. 20,000 copies were produced in Farsi, Arabic, Spanish and Portuguese and distributed to embassies, Government agencies and specifiers overseas.

A BCSA display stand was also developed for use at exhibitions, together with car stickers, a "Specify Steel" leaflet and regional specifier seminars. An audio-visual slide presentation was produced; in addition, BCSA's film, slide and photographic library was updated and re-organised.

Chapter Twelve - 1980 to 1990

Recession Bites

In the early 1980s, many companies invested heavily in new plant and buildings so that the industry would be well equipped for the next boom, then they suffered from unviable price-cutting as they strove to keep their workforce intact during the storm. The recession was seen as a challenge as well as a threat. Improved productivity, a high level of capital investment in workshop machinery and computer aids, more efficient management, closer attention to marketing – all contributed by the middle of the decade to a revival in confidence in steel in construction as a cost-effective and speedy solution to clients' requirements. There was a determination amongst steelwork fabricators to continue to improve competitiveness, to increase efficiency and to enlarge the available market.

As a result of BCSA lobbying, the Secretary of State for Transport agreed that 12 bridges would go out to tender based on dual designs – concrete and steel; steel won the vast majority of the tenders and this led to the growth in the use of steel for bridgework.

With considerable support from the British Steel Corporation's technical marketing campaigns, steel's popularity continued to grow. In the mid-1980s, the overall efficiency, competitiveness and quality of steel-framed construction became increasingly recognised. 1985 saw a large resurgence of interest in steel construction which was achieved not only because of fundamental economic factors, but also because of various technical innovations, such as profiled steel sheet decking, lightweight fire protection and the introduction of the BCSA/DTI sponsored FASTRAK 5950 suite of computer programs.

1985 also saw the industry's efforts to put its house in order by way of improvements in quality, responsible wage settlements, quick and reliable on-site erection. These were rewarded when, for the first time in over half of century, steel superseded in-situ concrete as the most popular form of construction for multi-storey buildings. There was a massive recovery in the quantity of steelwork fabricated, from 700,000 tonnes in 1983 to close on one million tonnes in 1986.

By the end of the 1980s, British Steel Corporation had been de-nationalised and had become an efficient steel producer by world standards of productivity.

In 1989, the industry's output peaked at a record 1.4 million tonnes.

Market Development

In 1984, BCSA re-started a promotion magazine with its new quarterly "BCSA News". The previous "Building with Steel" had been taken over by the British Steel Corporation and then soon ceased its publication. In 1986, the title of the new BCSA magazine was changed to "Steel Construction" and by 1988 was being issued six times per annum, with a distribution list of 13,000.

Press publicity began to be increased with special "steel construction" supplements in the trade and regional press, eg in the 'Yorkshire Post' and in the 'Birmingham Post'.

BCSA took an active role in the National Economic Development Organisation's (NEDO) Constructional Steelwork Economic Development Committee, which was active in the fields of research, education, promotion and relations with Government. A NEDO report on the "Efficiency of Multi-storey Buildings" was published in 1985.

Contractual

In 1984, BCSA launched its Liability Insurance Scheme for members and in 1985 published its Model Tendering Terms and Conditions for Steelwork Fabrication.

In addition to the regular local and regional members' meetings held throughout the country, in 1986 the programme of regular National Meetings was introduced, with one of the first being on "The Invisible Costs of Contracting" at which guest speakers discussed the fabrication industry's contractual problems.

Despite providing input into the drafting of the new Standard Method of Measurement section relating to structural steelwork (SMM7) which was published in 1989, BCSA's views were largely ignored. To alleviate the problem, the Association produced its own guidance notes to be used by quantity surveyors taking off steelwork bills.

Unreasonable warranties were a major problem and hence BCSA published its own standard form of connection warranty, which resulted in many clients agreeing to remove some of the more objectionable clauses.

Computer Applications

At the start of the decade, BCSA acquired several of the new microcomputers and instigated a loan scheme whereby members could borrow them "to demonstrate their capability as aids in the design, detailing and fabrication shop information". During 1982, over 40 member companies took part in the scheme.

The FASTRAK 5950 suite of programs commenced in 1984 under BCSA's direction for the design and estimating of multi-storey and portal framed buildings designed to BS 5950.

In 1987, BCSA conceived and instigated the pan-European Eureka project, which eventually resulted in the publication of the CIMsteel Integration Standards.

Technical

Demand for technical publications remained buoyant and many new books were published, eg "Manual on Connections", "Steel Bridges", "Erector's Manual", "Erection of Structural Steelwork", "International Structural Steelwork Handbook" and "Historical Structural Steelwork Handbook".

In 1989, the BCSA launched the National Structural Steelwork Specification for Building Construction (the "Black" Book) with the aim of achieving greater uniformity in contractual project specifications and eliminating the plethora of conflicting requirements which were faced by the industry. This necessitated extensive consultation and research, eg into the standards and level of inspection of welds.

The new limit state BS 5950 to supersede the permissible stress based BS 449 was finally published in August 1985. However, it was to be another 15 years before it effectively replaced BS 449.

In 1986, BCSA developed and launched the Quality Assurance Certification Scheme under the direction of an independent Governing Board. Also in 1986, CONSTRADO was "privatised" and became the Steel Construction Institute, an independent centre of technical excellence.

BCSA

In 1986, BCSA was granted the right to bear Arms. The basis of the design of the Coat of Arms is a helmet, which had been used by BCSA as its symbol in the early years. It is placed on a background of red lines, which are intended to represent a framework of girders. A lion is the basis of the crest – symbolising both the strength of steel and the nationality of the Association. The lion is spattered with bezants, suggestive of gold coins and frequently used in heraldry to represent commercial interests. The torch is intended to represent the information and research aspects of the Association's work. The lion is set within a circle of steel ingots. The motto is strength and stability – indicating both the strength and stability of the Association and of steel construction.

In response to numerous requests, and after lengthy consultation and discussion, 1987 saw an amendment to the BCSA's membership rules, which ratified the opening up of membership to other trading companies which subscribed to the BCSA's aims and objectives – such companies would be known as Associate Members.

In 1989, HRH The Princess Royal opened the Congress of the European Convention for Constructional Steelwork at Stratford-upon-Avon. The Congress, which was organised and hosted by BCSA, consisted of a three-day International Symposium, followed by the two-day Annual Meetings of ECCS, was attended by 500 people from 25 countries.

Since the establishment of its central London office, BCSA had been based in various rented offices around Victoria Street until 1989, when the lease was purchased on a suite of offices at 4 Whitehall Court, London SW1 in order to give the Association its permanent long-term headquarters.

Whitehall Court

Most of Whitehall was land given to the Royal Family of Scotland by the English Crown in c 800AD. The area became known as Scotland Yard and was the official residence of the Kings of Scotland in London. After the Palace of White Hall was destroyed by fire in 1698, private residences were built on the land. They were occupied through the years by well known historical figures, such as Inigo Jones and Sir Christopher Wren. Scotland Yard was the home of the Metropolitan Police Force from 1829 to 1966 when it moved to New Scotland Yard at St James.

Whitehall Court was built in 1895 and became the focus of the Liberator Building Society scandal. The property developer Jezebel Balfour created the building society as a vehicle for raising funds; he targeted vicars, persuading them to accept a small commission for recommending the society to their parishioners. Having built Whitehall Court as his showcase for his Building Society, he then ran off to South America with all of the funds!

Whitehall Court is in the style of a French Chateau and is listed as a building of architectural interest; its history has been enriched with the names of many famous residents: Henry Gladstone, Lord Kitchener, Grand Duke Michael of Russia, George Bernard Shaw, H G Wells and many others. During World War 1, it was used by the Secret Service, with most of the building being taken over by various Government departments from 1939 to 1946.

Chapter Thirteen - 1990 to 2000

Commercial

The early 1990s saw the industry in recession again. Not only was there a dramatic drop in the production of structural steelwork – from c 1.4 million tonnes in 1989 to 780,000 tonnes in 1992 – but prices also collapsed. All companies suffered greatly and many ceased trading. The industry, the backbone of construction, faced a difficult situation – attacked from all sides, unable to control its present and unable to plan its future. Most notably, companies in the steel construction sector suffered severely when several large London property developers got into trouble.

But even in the difficult times the industry continued to move forward; in the home market, steel's share of buildings of two or more storeys continued to increase. Exports saw a dramatic leap in the early 1990s, with companies proving that the UK has the world's best steel construction industry by winning orders all around the globe.

In anticipation of the Single European Market, member companies looked towards mainland Europe to develop their market potential and to increase their share of exported steelwork; to assist, BCSA produced a detailed Guide to Exporting Steelwork to Europe.

A major initiative in 1995 was the development and launch of the Register of Qualified Steelwork Contractors Scheme. This was more than just a list of companies, as each applicant company had to qualify by being audited by specialist auditors who check the company's financial and technical resources and track record. The Highways Agency quickly gave its endorsement by including in its tender documentation a requirement that only firms listed on the Register for the type and value of work to be undertaken would be employed for the fabrication and erection of bridgeworks.

The industry slowly recovered, such that by the end of the millennium, output was at 1.2 million tonnes and profitability was good.

Contractual

In 1992, an amendment to SMM7 came into force; this consisted of changes negotiated by BCSA to improve the steelwork section of the standard method.

By 1994, it was generally felt that an improvement in the industry's fortunes was on its way. Sir Michael Latham's review of procurement and contractual arrangements commenced and promised to be a watershed for the entire construction industry – starting a return to good practices that could only benefit the industry. Throughout 1995, members responded to the campaign to lobby their MPs to legislate against contractual and payment abuses; the success of this campaign led to the inclusion of construction legislation in the Queen's Speech in November 1995. Legislation was introduced into the House of Lords in February 1996 as part of the Housing, Grants, Construction and Regeneration Bill and received Royal Assent in July 1996.

The late 1990s saw improvements to the commercial environment with the elimination of cash retentions on steel construction contracts when BCSA registered an agreement with the Office of Fair Trading, whereby members agreed that they would not accept the deduction of cash retentions. Speaking at the BCSA's National Dinner in 1997, the Minister for Construction said: "I can well understand the difficulties that arise when sums of 3 or 5% of contract value are withheld by the client or main contractor in the form of retentions. At a time of tight margins, this element of cash flow can be particularly critical to the financial position of your businesses. The process can also limit investment and innovation. Helpfully, your Association has recognised that retention sums are not the only way to protect the interests of your clients and has introduced an insurance bond scheme. This sensible scheme has been an immediate success both with the industry and among clients. In the spirit of Latham, this scheme helps to remove a major source of confrontation – it is to be both applauded and recommended to other sectors."

At the end of the decade, although saddened by the demise of the Building Structures Group, BCSA was pleased to join the Specialist Engineering Contractors' Group.

Promotion

In 1991, BCSA launched its Steel Construction Challenge for Schools and new brochures were prepared to promote the industry. The Association's magazine was combined with SCI's magazine into a new bi-monthly publication "New Steel Construction" with a circulation list of 10,000.

The first National Steel Construction Week took place in October 1992, when over 3,000 delegates took part in 50 separate events around the country.

BCSA's first website – www.bcsa.org – was set up in 1996.

Directory for Specifiers & Buyers *1998*

STEEL CONSTRUCTION INDUSTRY

In 1998, the first "Directory for Specifiers and Buyers" was published to explain not only the capabilities of member companies, but also the competitive advantages of steel in construction.

In 1999, over 1,000 delegates from 26 countries came to London for BCSA's International Steel Construction Conference and Exhibition, culminating with a Millennium Banquet held at Guildhall with HRH The Princess Royal as the Principal Guest.

Technical

In 1991, the Construction Products Regulations were published to facilitate the introduction of CE marking – although it was to be another 15 years before this started to make an impact on the industry.

New books continued to be produced, for example "Moment Connections" in 1995. A "Commentary on

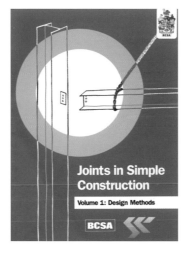

the National Structural Steelwork Specification" was first published in 1996, along with the first in a series of Health & Safety booklets.

A series of Government sponsored research projects was carried out looking at the future structure and direction of the industry.

The Association was active in a wide range of activities, including: wind loadings, stability during erection, simplification of EC3, fire, health & safety, CDM regulations, CAD/CAM, connections group, welding group, CNC users group, EPA group, etc.

BCSA worked closely with its colleagues in Corus (formerly British Steel) to develop the steel construction market and BCSA, Corus and SCI together started planning the design guides which would be necessary for a smooth transition to implement the Eurocodes.

BCSA

At the start of the decade BCSA, together with British Steel and SCI, formed the Steel Construction Industry Federation as a vehicle for closer working.

In 1992, the Association introduced its Fellowship Award for those individuals who had made an outstanding contribution and service to the industry.

1995 saw the launch of the Register of Qualified Steelwork Contractors Scheme, which was set up with the aim of improving competitiveness and efficiency in the steel construction industry by ensuring satisfaction, readily enabling identification of appropriate steelwork contractors and ensuring that competition takes place within a set level of competence and experience.

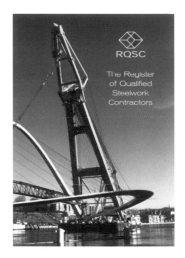

Overseas missions took place to Japan, China, South Africa, Italy and Brazil to learn from our sister industries worldwide and to seek out new export opportunities.

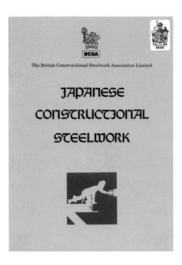

As part of the Association's strategic review, it was concluded that the two major aims to be pursued in the future would be to help improve members' business competence and their profitability.

In 1998, BCSA entered into a partnership with Macmillan Cancer Relief to help raise funds to support specialist doctors, nurses and buildings for cancer treatment and care.

A particular focus was placed on developing good relationships with Ministers and officials and in 1999, the Construction Minister said: "Without hesitation, I can say that your sector – and more specifically BCSA – is held in high regard within Government. The constructional steelwork sector is a vital element of the UK construction industry. Your sector has much to be proud of and I know you continue to look for opportunities for further innovation and development, developments in your products – developments in your methods of working. I cannot stress too highly how Government benefits from having a constructive dialogue with an industry that is innovative and forward looking – an industry that both responds to and informs customers' interests here in the UK and overseas. Your staff and members make an invaluable contribution to the development and implementation of new codes and standards".

Chapter Fourteen - 2000 to 2006

Commercial

The new millennium got off to a good start with steel showing its dominance as a framing material for multi-storey buildings, continuing with a market share of 69%. Steel was strong in all sectors, but showed its greatest dominance in the multi-storey industrial (92%), leisure (79%), retail (75%) and office (70%) fields; in no area did its share of the market fall significantly below 50%. In the non-domestic single-storey building market, steel enjoyed a market share of 90%. Speed of construction remained the number one reason for choosing steel, with "lowest overall cost" coming second.

2004 was a turbulent year for the steel construction industry, with frequent sharp increases in the price of our basic raw material – steel. The price increases were driven by global pressures on iron ore, coke and transport costs. The increases not only applied to steel sections, plate and strip, but also to reinforcing steel. During 2004, steel sections increased in price by around 50%. However, the price of rebar increased by 50% in the first three months of the year alone. Consequently, steel's competitive position over concrete for construction remained; for example, the cost of a steel beam and composite slab floor building frame was then around £90/m² compared with £150/m² for a reinforced concrete frame and flat slab and £175/m² for a concrete frame with a post tensioned flat slab.

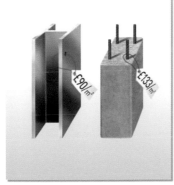

Mind the competitive gap

Despite the dramatic rise in steel prices during 2004, industry output and market share both increased and forward orders continued to be very healthy.

In 2005, steel prices were expected to be more stable, with price rises for steelwork anticipated to be of the order of 5 to 7%. Demand in UK was nearly as high as the all-time peak of 1.4 million tonnes in 1988/89: in 2004, output was 8% up on the previous year at 1.3 million tonnes. The industry continued to gain market share in a number of key sectors, such as residential, hospitals and education.

By 2006, BCSA members' forward order books were in a healthy situation and the latest independent report showed that steel's market share had reached an all time record high. Steel's share of the multi-storey non-residential buildings market had reached 70% for the first time; over the past 25 years, steel's market share had steadily increased from 25% to 70%.

The latest independent annual cost comparison study between steel frames and concrete once again proved that steel provides the most advantageous and economical framing solution. Although all construction products were facing raw material and energy price increases, steel, with the mills facing universal power/energy and raw material cost increases, was not the worst affected material. These pressures, combined with higher steel demand levels, lower stocks and higher prices in other regions of the world are resulted in the steel mills indicating that conditions were right for the mills to introduce higher market prices for structural sections. However, these section price increases, although significant, were thought unlikely to result in the price of fabricated steelwork increasing by more that 5% for 2006.

UK Consumption of Constructional Steelwork

																												FORECAST		
YEAR	79	80	81	82	83	84	85	86	87	88	89	90	91	92	93	94	95	96	97	98	99	00	01	02	03	04	05	06	07	08
SECTOR	Kt	Kt	Kt	Kt	Kt	Kt	Kt	Kt	Kt	Kt	Kt	Kt	Kt	Kt	Kt	Kt	Kt	Kt	Kt	Kt	Kt	Kt	Kt	Kt	Kt	Kt	Kt	Kt	Kt	Kt
Industrial	689	584	440	400	358	459	563	495	580	658	745	620	425	398	431	504	559	578	644	643	631	616	600	530	502	575	567	566	560	558
Offices (Private)	(See notes 1 and 2 below)											164	125	96	86	82	89	99	109	121	145	164	186	170	148	133	140	149	157	165
Offices (Public)	(See notes 1 and 2 below)											18	17	15	16	18	15	12	10	10	11	10	10	16	18	18	16	13	11	10
Offices Total	(See notes 1 and 2 below)											182	142	111	102	100	104	111	119	131	156	174	196	186	166	151	156	162	168	175
Retail	(See notes 1 and 2 below)											77	81	71	70	88	82	92	95	102	106	99	101	115	125	129	123	123	124	126
Leisure	(See note 2 below)											63	51	44	41	52	54	65	92	103	108	103	90	90	81	93	87	82	87	90
Health	(See note 1 below)											11	10	11	14	14	14	11	12	13	14	16	16	18	20	28	28	27	29	31
Education	(See note 1 below)											9	9	10	13	16	19	18	17	19	22	27	34	41	47	54	56	58	60	63
Generation	19	32	33	31	18	12	15	10	10	12	12	27	27	23	22	18	14	15	16	19	18	16	15	16	17	17	19	21	24	26
Towers	3	4	4	5	6	6	4	3	3	1	2	2	3	4	3	3	5	5	3	5	4	5	4	4	4	4	5	5	5	6
Power Total	22	36	37	36	24	18	19	13	13	13	14	29	30	27	25	21	19	20	19	24	22	21	19	20	21	21	24	26	29	32
Bridges	17	12	16	14	14	21	23	25	47	52	57	47	47	49	51	59	49	38	34	28	27	29	31	36	42	28	28	32	33	34
Other Infrastructure	(See note 3 below)															8	10	14	20	24	25	26	28	28	44	44	31	29	26	26
Domestic	6	4	2	2	3	3	2	2	3	5	8	6	6	6	6	6	6	6	6	8	10	12	15	20	30	52	53	53	52	50
Agriculture	92	88	77	82	99	93	105	65	70	64	61	60	49	47	52	54	52	47	47	46	45	43	35	41	45	50	51	53	54	56
Other	(See note 2 below)											29	24	16	18	19	23	28	33	33	37	36	35	33	37	38	39	40	41	42
Fabricated Exports	100	65	95	115	93	90	80	59	52	46	49	54	57	65	65	68	87	67	72	78	66	68	88	85	95	85	91	85	80	80
TOTAL UK PRODUCTION	1081	938	831	829	790	920	1054	976	1148	1286	1427	1189	931	855	888	1009	1078	1095	1210	1252	1269	1270	1288	1243	1255	1348	1334	1336	1343	1363
Year-on-Year % Change	-	-13.2	-11.4	-0.2-	4.7	16.5	14.6	-7.4	17.6	12.0	11.0	-16.7	-21.7	-8.2	3.9	13.6	6.8	1.6	10.5	3.5	1.4	0.1	1.4	-3.5	1.0	7.4	-1.0	0.1	0.5	1.5

NOTES
1. Commercial and Public tonnages were not split until 1990.
2. Commercial tonnage was also sub-divided into new categories - Leisure and Other - from 1990.
3. Other Infrastructure tonnage was not identified separately before 1994.

Steel vs Concrete - cost comparison

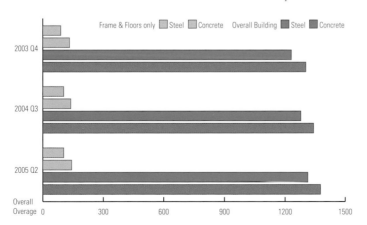

Steel's growing market share

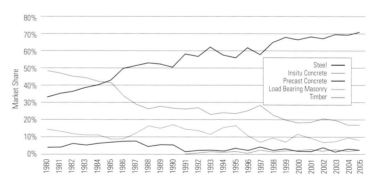

Figures supplied by Corus Group plc and BCSA

Contractual

Through its contacts in Government, BCSA was instrumental in obtaining a statement in the March 2004 Budget that a review would take place of the operation of the adjudication and payment provisions in the Construction Act in order to identify what improvements can be made to change the situation regarding the unreasonable delays in payment which members suffer in construction contracts.

It is hoped that this Review will deliver results: BCSA is pleased that the DTI now accepts that there is a problem as far as certainty of payment is concerned and that action is needed to ensure that the vital lifeblood of the industry – cash – flows more smoothly in future. Money is not everything, but it is extremely difficult to live without it.

Timely and detailed project information is another issue which affects all and, together with other organisations such as the Association for Consultancy and Engineering, BCSA is aiming to produce a new document for steelwork alongside the National Structural Steelwork Specification which will set out guidance on information requirements.

Health and Safety

A key theme of BCSA is health and safety. The reality of life is that, regrettably, accidents will and do happen, but all must recognise this and work together to reduce, if not eliminate, the risk of accidents, no matter where they are likely to occur. Safety is our collective responsibility. The health and safety of all the people involved in the industry was therefore placed at the top of BCSA's agenda. To this end, BCSA was active in a variety of areas, both on and off site – publishing new guides, liaising with HSE and researching the causes of accidents.

In 2002, the Minister with responsibility for Health and Safety in Construction launched BCSA's "Safer Steel Construction" programme. This was a wide package of measures, including the Safe Site Handover Certificate, which quickly gained acceptance amongst the leading main contractors as the standard setting requirement for the safe sites. The following year saw the launch the new BCSA "Erector Cards", jointly with the Construction Skills Certification Scheme.

In 2004, new best practice guides were prepared for the safe erection of low rise buildings, metal decking and stud welding, bridges, and erecting steelwork in windy conditions. The Steel Construction Certification Scheme extended its scope to certification services for health and safety, in addition to quality management and environmental management.

Two more best practice guides were planned for publication in 2006 – one on the erection of Multi-Storey Buildings and one on the Loading and Unloading of Trailers.

Technical

The tragic events of 11 September 2001, leading to the destruction of the World Trade Center towers, will never be forgotten. The official US report published in May 2002 said: "The structural damage sustained by each of the two buildings as a result of the terrorist attacks was massive.

The fact that the structures were able to sustain this level of damage and remain standing for an extended period of time is remarkable and is the reason that most building occupants were able to evacuate safely." BCSA co-operated in the reviews of the design of such tall structures, covering aspects such as: means of escape, robustness, connection design and fire protection.

With regard to safety in use, it is a fact that structural frames, whether they be steel, concrete or timber, need to be designed to resist fire and by 2003 an extensive programme of full-scale fire tests had been successfully carried out on the steel frame at Cardington. BCSA put forward the view that all new forms of construction for frames and floors in all materials should be extensively fire tested.

Computers played increasingly important roles to facilitate accuracy and ease of transfer of data, with 3D product modelling and the developing use of a 'single project model' helping to move the construction industry forward.

With the Eurocodes coming, BCSA was doing all it could, together with its partners Corus and SCI, to help with implementation in order to ensure steel structures continued to be easy and economic to design. For example, National Annexes and design aids for Eurocode 3 and 4 were under development.

CE marking for fabricated steelwork would probably be introduced in 2007 and members were encouraged to be open to accept this new approach.

However, it was considered vital for the construction industry as a whole and its clients that British Standards should be maintained until such time as the new Eurocodes and their supporting documents had been demonstrated to be user friendly, unambiguous and resulted in safe and economic structures. It was unlikely that the full package of Eurocode documents would be available until 2008 — hence the planned withdrawal of British Standards in 2010 was far too early and needed to be extended.

Marketing

The Minister for e-Commerce launched BCSA's new website at the National Dinner held at the Savoy Hotel in 2001, when she said:

"The BCSA is an important part of the culture of continuous improvement, innovation and best practice, for example on e-commerce. I am delighted to announce the launch of the industry's new internet portal www.SteelConstruction.org. The new site will enable clients and specifiers to find information about steel construction companies and suppliers to the steel construction industry and also to search for advice and information about steel construction related topics. It will also enable the staff in BCSA member companies to gain access, via a password, to an extensive information resource not available to non-member companies."

A new supplement, "Steel Construction News", was launched, the circulation of which was to grow into over 100,000 – the biggest of any publication in the construction industry – by way of inserts into the leading trade magazines.

In 2002, a highly successful bridge conference attended by 240 delegates was held at the Institution of Civil Engineers to launch the new "Steel Bridges" book.

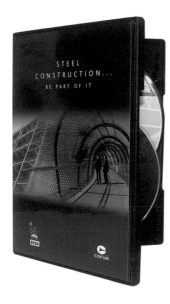

BCSA continued to disseminate best practice guidance and in 2003 over 300 delegates attended the Steel Buildings Conference and Exhibition. At the Conference, a new comprehensive book on "Steel Buildings" was published. Increased promotion took place during 2003/4 with full page advertisements in the press showing examples of steel-framed hospitals, multi-storey residential buildings, schools and car parks. A further Conference and Exhibition took place in 2005 with the publication of a new "Steel Details" book.

In 2004, the first of a new annual "Steel Construction – Be Part Of It" pack was sent to almost 10,000 university undergraduates, comprising an introductory booklet about steel construction together with explanatory CDs.

Co-operation

Whilst continuing the co-operation with European colleagues via ECCS, BCSA extended this dialogue with its English speaking sister organisations worldwide. A joint meeting took place in 2004 between BCSA (UK), AISC (USA), CISC (Canada), ASI (Australia), SAISC (South Africa) and HERA (New Zealand) in California. The objective of this new International Steelwork Contractors Group (ISCG) was to gain ideas from each country for new market development initiatives; discussions took place on: marketing, fire, 3D modelling, IT, and visions for the future. The second ISCG meeting took place in York, England in 2005.

Through the Specialist Engineering Contractors Group (SECG), BCSA co-operates with the other specialist engineering contracting sectors to develop better payment and contractual terms; the review of the Construction Act is one result of this co-operation. Through the Metals Forum (an umbrella body covering 500,000 employees), BCSA works with other trade associations to raise the profile of the metals manufacturing and processing industries and to identify new European legislation which will impact on member companies.

New Initiatives

In 2005, the Steel Construction Sustainability Charter was launched, the objective of which was to develop steel as a sustainable form of construction in terms of economic viability, social progress and environmental responsibility. BCSA required that Sustainability Charter members made a formal declaration to operate their businesses in efficient and financially sustainable ways in order to undertake contracts that satisfy clients and add value for stakeholders. BCSA would be auditing Charter member companies and planned to develop and publish key performance indicators that benchmark the development of sustainable steel construction generally and that permit individual Sustainability Charter members to measure their own progress.

In 2006, there were many more important initiatives and activities under way, such as:

- a review of industrial training with Metskill/SEMTA;
- improved contacts with Universities and students;
- new certification activities by SCCS;
- a review of BCSA membership entry requirements and benefits;
- new technical guidance documents, for example on galvanising;
- a bigger promotion drive via "New Steel Construction" magazine;
- the flagship Structural Design Awards Scheme.

Centenary

A Centenary Dinner was held at the Savoy Hotel, London on 7 March 2006 attended by 450 members, their guests and guests of the Association. The Principal Guest, The Minister for Industry, Construction and the Regions, congratulated the BCSA on its Centenary, saying that the industry's achievements are all around us and that "steel is now more than ever the material of choice". He added that, over the past 100 years, steel construction has become an indispensable part of construction and that the industry had a history to be proud of, eg Tower Bridge, Hong Kong Airport and Terminal 5 to give just a few examples. BCSA members also build structures for everyday life, such as hospitals, distribution centres, and industrial buildings.

In association with BCSA's Centenary, the Financial Times published its first Special Report on Steel Construction: http://news.ft.com/reports/steelconstruction2006

Over 130,000 copies of the report were printed and included in the newspaper on 8 March 2006.

The Association's Centenary Banquet was held at Blenheim Palace on 16 June 2006 attended by 460 member company representatives, past Presidents, Fellows and staff.

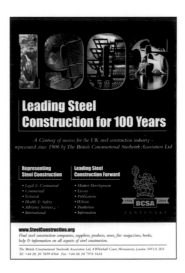

But what of the future ...?

Steel's success is ultimately down to member companies. The Minister for Industry said in 2005 at the Seminar for Residential Clients and Developers:

"If we are to deliver a world-class built environment, companies along the supply chain will need to work much closer together. I know that the BCSA is encouraging its members to work with clients in particular to ensure that a solution is developed as much as possible pre-construction, so that re-working, which is so wasteful, is eliminated.

"BCSA members use advanced production technology — for example CAD programs and computer-controlled cutting, punching and welding — and have an excellent understanding of how to produce detailed designs, using steel as a structural material, for any given project. Continuous investment allied to innovative thinking has created a new range of multi-storey buildings and modular structures, which in turn have opened up new markets for the steelwork industry. Not to mention the benefits of reduced time and increased safety on site and less disruption in the surrounding area.

"The BCSA is to be congratulated for its efforts to foster innovation, raise standards and improve performance within the sector."

The Industry's future lies in the hands of individual members and it is for them to carry the success onwards. The BCSA can commission surveys, publish books, institute comparison schemes, instigate new initiatives and take many other steps for the benefit of members, but it is the industry itself which must act, take advantage of what is offered and ensure that the BCSA continues to serve its members to best advantage.

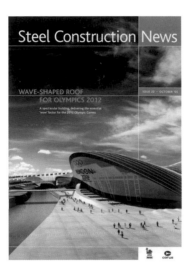

Looking forward, the hosting of the 2012 Olympics should also prove to be of great benefit to the industry and should increase demand by about 5% over each of the next five years.

BCSA Group Structure

BCSA Limited

MEMBERS OF THE COUNCIL

Office Bearers

D McCormack	President
R B Barrett	Deputy President
T G Goldberg	Immediate Past President

Midland and Southern Region

R N Harrison	A G Hernon

Northern Region

A J Holmes	G J Badge

Scottish Region

J H Sanderson	J G Kirkpatrick

Northern Ireland Region

E Fisher	D Watson

Bridgework Conference

P Miller	B Rogan

VICE PRESIDENTS

W L Fletcher CBE	B D Farmer	B T Shuttleworth	A F Collins
W R Cox MBE	J Locke MBE	D F Bingham	B F Hoppé OBE
A A H Bone	J A Humphryes	P R Samworth	S G Fareham
D H Peters OBE	G C Barrett OBE		

Co-opted Council Member

Dr J M Roberts

Vice Presidents

P R Samworth	S G Fareham

Committee Chairmen

S Boyd	Commercial and Contracts
A H Pillinger	Process and Technical
E S Price	Health and Safety
G H Taylor	Marketing and Membership Services

Director General

Dr D Tordoff

Secretary

Mrs M C Rich

The British Constructional Steelwork Association Limited

DIRECTORS

D McCormack	President	T G Goldberg	Immediate Past President
R B Barrett	Deputy President	Mrs M C Rich	Company Secretary

HEAD OFFICE

Director General	D Tordoff BSc PhD CEng FICE FRSA FInstD FCMI MIHT
Deputy Director General	Miss G M Mitchell MBE
Director, Legal & Contractual Affairs	Mrs M C Rich Barrister MSc FCIArb
Director of Engineering	D B Moore CEng BTech PhD MIStructE
Health & Safety Manager	P Walker CFIOSH
Accounts Manager	D A Thornicroft BA
Technical Consultant	R J Pope MA MSc DPhil CEng FIMechE FIStructE MCIArb

REGISTER OF QUALIFIED STEELWORK CONTRACTORS SCHEME

Auditors	J E Evans BSc(Eng) Hons ACGI DIC CEng FICE FIWeldI FACE FRSA
	M T Hamilton MRICS
	R J Pope MA MSc DPhil CEng FIMechE FIStructE MCIArb

Steel Construction Certification Scheme Limited

DIRECTORS

D McCormack	R B Barrett
T G Goldberg	Mrs M C Rich (Company Secretary)

CERTIFICATION BOARD

Chairman of the Certification Board

D A Woodward

HEAD OFFICE

Scheme Manager	P R Mould MIQA Registered Lead Auditor
Scheme Assessors	Dr R Cheesman PhD FIQA MRSC ChChem Registered Lead Auditor
	S Mills CEI BA Registered Lead Auditor (IRCA & RAB)
	D Taylor CEng MIMechE Principal Auditor IEMA

BCSA Regional Secretaries

Midland and Southern Region
Ms L Carlisle
74 Rowan Way, Balderton
Newark NG24 3BJ
Tel: 01636 681321   Fax: 01636 681321

Scottish Region
S Henderson
34 Torwood Brae, Earnock
Hamilton ML3 9XB
Tel: 01698 422429   Fax: 01698 422804

Northern Region
M Hamilton
30 Derby Road, Ansdell
Lytham St Annes FY8 4BZ
Tel: 01253 736857   Fax: 0870 1244972

Northern Ireland Region
T Wylie
27 Glenariff Park, Bangor
Co Down BT20 4UY
Tel: 028 9146 7454   Fax: 028 9127 0508

Company	Telephone
ACL Structures Ltd	01258 456051
A & J Fabtech Ltd	01924 402151
ASA Steel Structures Ltd	01782 566366
Adey Steel Ltd	01509 556677
Adstone Construction Ltd	01905 794561
Allerton Engineering Ltd	01609 774471
Allott Bros & Leigh	01709 364115
Allslade plc	023 9266 7531
The Angle Ring Co Ltd	0121 557 7241
Apex Steel Structures Ltd	01268 660828
Arbuckle Welding & Fabrications Ltd	01236 457960
Arromax Structures Ltd	01623 747466
Asme Engineering Ltd	020 8954 0028
Atlas Ward Structures Ltd	01944 710421
Atlasco Constructional Engineers Ltd	01782 564711
B D Structures Ltd	01942 817770
BHC Ltd	01555 840006
A C Bacon Engineering Ltd	01953 850611
Ballykine Structural Engineers Ltd	028 9756 2560
Barnshaw Section Benders Ltd	0121 557 8261
Barrett Steel Buildings Ltd	01274 266800
Barretts of Aspley Ltd	01525 280136
Billington Structures Ltd	01226 340666
Billington Structures Ltd	01454 314201
Bison Structures Ltd	01666 502792
Bone Steel Ltd	01698 375000
F J Booth & Partners Ltd	01642 241581
Border Steelwork Structures Ltd	01228 548744
Bourne Steel Ltd	01202 746666
W S Britland & Co Ltd	01304 831583
Briton Fabricators Ltd	0115 963 2901
Browne Structures Ltd	01283 212720
Butterley Ltd	01773 573573
Cairnhill Structures Ltd	01236 449393
Caunton Engineering Ltd	01773 531111
Chieftain Contracts Ltd	01324 812911
Cleveland Bridge UK Ltd	01325 381188
Compass Engineering Ltd	01226 298388
Conder Structures Ltd	01283 545377
Leonard Cooper Ltd	0113 270 5441
Cordell Group Ltd	01642 452406
Coventry Construction Ltd	024 7646 4484
Crown Structural Engineering Ltd	01623 490555
Custom Metal Fabrications Ltd	020 8844 0940
DGT Steel & Cladding Ltd	01603 308200
D H Structures Ltd	01785 246269
Frank H Dale Ltd	01568 612212
Dew Construction Ltd	0161 624 5361
Elland Steel Structures Ltd	01422 380262
Emmett Fabrications Ltd	01274 597484
EvadX Ltd	01745 336413
Fairfield-Mabey Ltd	01291 623801
Fisher Engineering Ltd	028 6638 8521
GME Structures Ltd	01939 233023
Gibbs Engineering Ltd	01278 455253
Glentworth Fabrications Ltd	0118 977 2088
Gorge Fabrications Ltd	0121 522 5770
Graham Wood Structural Ltd	01903 755991
Grays Engineering (Contracts) Ltd	01375 372411
D A Green & Sons Ltd	01406 370585
Gregg & Patterson (Engineers) Ltd	028 9061 8131
Had-Fab Ltd	01875 611711
William Haley Engineering Ltd	01278 760591
Hambleton Steel Ltd	01748 810598
William Hare Ltd	0161 609 0000
M Hasson & Sons Ltd	028 2957 1281
Hawkes Construction Company	01708 621010
Hescott Engineering Company Ltd	01324 556610
Hillcrest Structural Ltd	023 8064 1373
Hills of Shoeburyness Ltd	01702 296321
Horwich Steelworks Ltd	01204 695989
James Bros (Hamworthy) Ltd	01202 673815
Joy Steel Structures (London) Ltd	020 7474 0550
James Killelea & Co Ltd	01706 229411
T A Kirkpatrick & Co Ltd	01461 800275
Leach Structural Steelwork Ltd	01995 640133
Lowe Engineering (Midland) Ltd	01889 563244
M D Fabrications Ltd	01633 266691
M&S Engineering Ltd	01461 40111
Maldon Marine Ltd	01621 859000
Harry Marsh (Engineers) Ltd	0191 510 9797
Terence McCormack Ltd	028 3026 2261
Midland Steel Structures Ltd	024 7644 5584
Mifflin Construction Ltd	01568 613311
Newbridge Engineering Ltd	01429 866722
Newton Fabrications Ltd	01292 269135
Nusteel Structures Ltd	01303 268112
On Site Services (Gravesend) Ltd	01474 321552
Overdale Construction Services Ltd	01656 729229
PMS Fabrications Ltd	01228 599090
Harry Peers Steelwork Ltd	01204 528393
Pencro Structural Engineering Ltd	028 9335 2886
QMEC Ltd	01246 822228
RSL (South West) Ltd	01460 67373
John Reid & Sons (Structsteel) Ltd	01202 483333
Remnant Engineering Ltd	01594 841160
Rippin Ltd	01388 518610
Roberts Engineering	01482 838240
J Robertson & Company Ltd	01255 672855
Robinson Construction	01332 574711
Rowecord Engineering Ltd	01633 250511
Rowen Structures Ltd	01623 558558
S H Structures Ltd	01977 681931
Selwyn Construction Engineering Ltd	0151 678 0236
Severfield-Reeve Structures Ltd	01845 577896
Shipley Fabrications Ltd	01400 231115
Henry Smith (Constructional Engineers) Ltd	01606 592121
Snashall Steel Fabrications Co Ltd	01300 345588
South Durham Structures Ltd	01388 777350
Taylor & Russell Ltd	01772 782295
The AA Group Ltd	01695 50123
The Steel People Ltd	01622 715900
Traditional Structures Ltd	01922 414172
W I G Engineering Ltd	01869 320515
Warley Construction Company Ltd	01268 726020
Walter Watson Ltd	028 4377 8711
Watson Steel Structures Ltd	01204 699999
Westbury Park Engineering Ltd	01373 825500
Westok Ltd	01924 264121
John Wicks & Son Ltd	01364 72907
H Young Structures Ltd	01953 601881

Associate Members

Company	Telephone
ASD metal services - Edinburgh	0131 459 3200
ASD metal services - Bodmin	01208 77066
ASD metal services - London	020 7476 0444
ASD metal services - Carlisle	01228 674766
ASD metal services - Hull	01482 633360
ASD metal services - Grimsby	01472 353851
ASD metal services - Biddulph	01782 515152
ASD metal services - Durham	0191 492 2322
ASD metal services - Cardiff	029 2046 0622
ASD metal services - Stalbridge	01963 362646
ASD metal services - Norfolk	01553 761431
ASD metal services - Exeter	01395 233366
ASD metal services - Daventry	01327 876021
ASD metal services - Tividale	0121 520 1231
Advanced Steel Services Ltd	01772 259822
Albion Sections Ltd	0121 553 1877
Alternative Steel Co Ltd	01942 610601
Ameron International	01623 511000
Arro-Cad Ltd	01283 558206
Austin Trumanns Steel Ltd	0161 790 4821
Ayrshire Metal Products (Daventry) Ltd	01327 300990
Barnshaw Plate Bending Centre Ltd	0161 320 9696
Barrett Steel Services Ltd	01274 682281
Brown McFarlane Ltd	01782 289909
Brunswick Steel Services	01724 810811
Caledonia Draughting Ltd	01738 560501
Cellbeam Ltd	01937 840614
Celtic Steel Services	01443 812181
Combisafe International Ltd	01604 660600
Composite Profiles UK Ltd	01202 659237
Computer Services Consultants (UK) Ltd	0113 239 3000
Corus Colors	01244 892309
Corus Construction & Industrial	01724 404040
Corus Panels & Profiles	01684 856600
Corus Research Development & Technology	01709 820166
Corus Tubes	01536 402121
Corus Service Centre - Blackburn	01254 55161
Corus Service Centre - Bristol	01454 315314
Corus Service Centre - Dartford	01322 227272
Corus Service Centre - Glasgow	0141 959 1212
Corus Service Centre - Grantham	01476 565522
Corus Service Centre - Leeds	0113 276 0660
Corus Service Centre - Northern Ireland	028 9266 0747
Corus Service Centre - Wednesfield	01902 484100
Development Design Detailing Services Ltd	01204 396606
Dudley Iron & Steel Co Ltd	0121 601 5000
Easi-Edge	01777 870901
FLI Products	01452 722260
Fabsec Ltd	0113 385 7830
Ficep (UK) Ltd	0113 265 3921
Forward Protective Coatings Ltd	01623 748323
Hi Span Ltd	01953 603081
Intelligent Engineering (UK) Ltd	01753 890575
International Paint Ltd	0191 469 6111
Kaltenbach Ltd	01234 213201
Kingspan Metl-Con Ltd	01944 712000
Richard Lees Steel Decking Ltd	01335 300999
Leigh's Paints	01204 521771
MSW Structural Floor Systems	0115 946 2316
Metsec plc	0121 601 6001
National Tube Stockholders Ltd	01845 577440
Newton Steel Stock Ltd	01963 365028
Odda Design Ltd	01474 352849
Peddinghaus Corporation UK Ltd	01952 200377
Portway Steel Services	01454 311442
Psycle Interactive Ltd	01948 780120
RAM International (Europe) Ltd	0141 353 5168
Rainham Steel Co Ltd	01708 522311
Rösler UK	0151 482 0444
Sigma Coatings Ltd	01525 375234
Site Coat Services Ltd	01476 577473
South Park Steel Services	01925 245511
South Park Steel Services	01724 810810
Steelstock (Burton-on-Trent) Ltd	01283 226161
Structural Metal Decks Ltd	01425 471088
Structural Sections Ltd	0121 555 1342
Struthers & Carter Ltd	01482 795171
Studwelders Ltd	01291 626048
Tekla (UK) Ltd	0113 307 1200
Jack Tighe Ltd	01302 880360
Voortman UK Ltd	01827 63300
Wedge Group Galvanizing Ltd	01909 486384

Corporate Members

Company	Telephone
Balfour Beatty Power Networks Ltd	01332 661491
Griffiths & Armour	0151 236 5656
Highways Agency	08457 504030
Roger Pope Associates	01752 263636

BCSA Limited

The British Constructional Steelwork Association was originally formed in 1906 as the Steelwork Society; other regional organisations were formed in the succeeding years and these came together in 1936 as BCSA.

Presidents

1936 - 1946	H Cunningham	1978 - 1979	D H Peters OBE
1946 - 1950	J W Baillie	1979 - 1981	B D Farmer
1950 - 1954	C Hipwell	1981 - 1983	W R Cox MBE
1954 - 1957	T S Gibson	1983 - 1986	G C Barrett OBE
1957 - 1959	J Brown	1986 - 1988	B T Shuttleworth
1959 - 1961	W H Vickers	1988 - 1990	J Locke MBE
1961 - 1962	W M Watson	1990 - 1992	A A H Bone
1962 - 1964	A S Nicholas	1992 - 1994	A F Collins
1964 - 1965	T S Gibson	1994 - 1996	D F Bingham
1965 - 1968	J D Bolckow CBE	1996 - 1998	B F Hoppé OBE
1968 - 1970	R B Denton	1998 - 2000	P R Samworth
1970 - 1972	J W Rankin	2000 - 2003	S G T Fareham
1972 - 1975	W L Fletcher CBE	2003 - 2005	T G Goldberg
1975 - 1978	J A Humphries	2005 -	D McCormack

Directors General

1936 - 1940	J Halliday
1940 - 1965	L P Bacon
1965 - 1979	D D ffrench
1980 - 1984	J C T Hackett
1984 -	D Tordoff